10 GREAT DATES

to

ENERGIZE

your marriage

Resources by David and Claudia Arp

Books

10 Great Dates for Empty Nesters

10 Great Dates Before You Say "I Do"
(co-authored with Curt and Natelle Brown)

10 Great Dates: Connecting Faith, Love and Marriage
(co-authored with Heather and Peter Larson)

$10 Great Dates
(co-authored with Heather and Peter Larson)

52 Fantastic Dates for You and Your Mate

The Second Half of Marriage

Fighting for Your Empty Nest Marriage
(co-authored with Scott Stanley, Howard Markman,
and Susan Blumberg)

No Time for Sex

She's Almost a Teenager — Essential Conversations to Have Now
(co-authored with Heather and Peter Larson)

The Connected Family

Answering the 8 Cries of the Spirited Child

Video Curriculum

10 Great Dates to Energize Your Marriage

10 Great Dates Before You Say "I Do"
(with Heather and Peter Larson)

Great Dates Connect
(with Heather and Peter Larson)

10 GREAT DATES

to

ENERGIZE

your marriage

UPDATED AND EXPANDED EDITION

DAVID & CLAUDIA ARP

ZONDERVAN®

ZONDERVAN

10 Great Dates to Energize Your Marriage
Copyright © 1997, 2016 by David and Claudia Arp

Requests for information should be addressed to:
Zondervan, 3900 *Sparks Drive SE, Grand Rapids, Michigan* 49546

This edition: ISBN 978-0-310-34402-5

10 Great Dates is a registered trademark.

Throughout the book names have been changed.

This book is a resource for marriage enrichment, not a substitute for needed professional counseling. If some of the exercises in this book raise issues for you or your spouse that cannot be easily resolved, we urge you to seek professional help.

Published in association with the literary agency of Alive Communications, Inc., 7680 Goddard Street, Suite 200, Colorado Springs, CO 80920.

Cover design: Connie Gabbert | design + illustration
Interior design: Denise Froehlich

First printing January 2016 / Printed in the United States of America

To the many couples who over the years
have experienced *10 Great Dates* and shared
your experiences with us

Contents

PART ONE: 10 GREAT DATES

PART TWO: YOUR DATING GUIDE

Acknowledgments

We gratefully acknowledge the contributions of the following people:

- Those who have pioneered marriage education and on whose shoulders we stand, including David and Vera Mace, John Gottman, David Olson, Sherod Miller, Dianne Sollee, and our friends at PREP (Prevention and Relationship Enhancement Program), including Scott Stanley, Howard Markman, and Susan Blumberg.
- The many other researchers and authors we quoted, for your sound work, which gives a solid base for the cause of marriage enrichment.
- Others who shared their stories and insights, including Aaron Larson, Harriet McManus, and Bethany Johnson.
- The many couples who have attended our seminars and experienced their own *10 Great Dates*, for your comments and input.
- Our editor, Sandy Vander Zicht, for sharing your expertise and patiently nudging us on.
- Our production editor, Jim Ruark.
- Our marketing director, Alicia Mey Kasen.
- Our literary agent, Greg Johnson, for being our advocate and encouraging us along the way.

A Personal Note

Have you ever gone kayaking with your spouse or a friend? If so, you know how easily kayaks can drift away from each other if you simply allow the water currents to push you along. Staying together requires effort—intentional paddling and steering. And it's likely no surprise to you that the same principle applies to marriage. There are many challenges in the river of life. It is infinitely easier to meet those challenges if you and your spouse are paddling and steering together—and infinitely harder to do so when you've drifted apart. That's just one of the reasons it's important to have an intentional way to steer your boats back together again.

We've never been brave enough to try kayaking, but we have experienced whitewater rafting and lived to tell the tale. At first it was so easy and fun—we just floated downstream. All seemed so calm and pleasant that we were lulled into a naïve confidence and thought, "Hey, we can handle this! What's so hard about whitewater rafting?" However, when the water currents abruptly sped up, our lazy floating experience suddenly became a hair-raising fight for survival! We had to work together to steer our raft away from sharp rocks, stay upright, and try to slow the pace. We somehow made it through without capsizing, and only later learned that the rapids we'd just survived were aptly named, "Devil Shoals." We were very happy to finish the course and get our feet back on solid ground.

Navigating the Rapids

Navigating the whitewater challenges of building a marriage is a lot like shooting the rapids. Developing skills for the "devil shoals" of life will make a big difference in how you handle what may be waiting just around the next bend in your relationship. Over the years we've taught thousands of couples how to develop these skills—and how to put new energy, excitement, and romance into their relationship—by having focused, fun dates. In the following pages you'll not only learn new skills that will help you in the future but you'll also discover just how fun dating your spouse can be.

Think about some of your past great dates. We bet they involved adventure and maybe even some risk. One of our most exciting dates was flying over the glaciers and ice fields of the Alaskan Kenai Peninsula in a small, six-seater twin-engine Cessna. Certainly this was one date neither of us ever considered! Some call it "flight-seeing"; I (Claudia) renamed it "fright-seeing."

While dating is a habit we've had for years, we never know where we will end up on a date. Our "flight-seeing" date started when our friend Eileen asked us, "How would you like to experience a great date in Alaska?" Being an adventurous couple, we responded, "Wow! How do we sign up?"

The next thing we knew, we were on a plane headed to Anchorage, Alaska. Of course there was a catch—while in Alaska we agreed to lead several marriage and family seminars. That's where we met another dating couple, Kyle and Ashley, who had found our book several years ago, and told us their story.

"After a lackluster first ten years of marriage, we both agreed we needed to jazz up our relationship," Kyle said, "but we weren't sure how to go about it."

"That's when I found your book," Ashley said. "Kyle wasn't so sure dating would help us—he was the original 'reluctant spouse.' But after some friendly persuasion, he agreed to try."

Kyle nodded. "I was hesitant for sure," he said. "We'd tried working through other marriage manuals but it didn't help much. I'm a teacher, and the last thing I wanted was more assignments and work. But I have to admit, these dates were different—they were fun, and we picked up some new skills that pushed our relationship a couple of notches higher."

Time to Take It Up a Notch

Are you looking for that little something extra to push your relationship a few notches higher? Want to heat up your connection to the sizzling point? You don't have to go all the way to Alaska to add excitement, but you do need to set aside some time to be together. When was the last time you had an uninterrupted thirty-minute conversation with your spouse? Would you like to have more fun together? Is dating something you did only before you were married or before you had kids? Has the chronic stress of overload crept into your lives? Maybe you don't feel as connected as you used to be. Perhaps you feel you're drifting apart and even falling out of love. You can't remember the last time you had an in-depth conversation or laughed together or did something spontaneous. Your kayaks aren't even close and you're feeling alone. If you relate to any of these statements, great dates can help you reconnect.

Having a growing relationship requires friendship, fun, and romance, and we've discovered there's no better way to encourage all of these than having dates! Great dates are more than going to see a movie and tuning out the world for a while. Great dates involve communicating, reviving the spark that initially ignited your fire, and developing mutual interests and goals that have nothing to do with your careers or your children.

If you're intrigued but still skeptical, we've got proof! We have worked hard on our own marriage. Through our own successes and failures and through research and study, we discovered principles that helped us build a strong marriage partnership. Amazingly, we found that one key indicator of an enriched marriage is having a strong "couple" friendship. And what better way to build a great couple friendship than to date your spouse?

Here's what a few other couples say about their *10 Great Dates* experience:

- *We had been married for less than a year when we found your book and started dating. As newlyweds, we had not continued the dating habit. After all, we were together in the evenings. Why should we have dates? Then a friend gave us your book and we decided to try it out. We decided it couldn't hurt to read it even if we thought we didn't need it. Through our ten dates, we learned upfront how to communicate better and manage our differences.*

- *One of the best things we did for our relationship in the early years of our marriage was developing the habit of regular date nights. Five years and two babies later, we're still dating, and our dates continue to give us the opportunity to step out of our hectic life and work on improving our marriage. Plus, dating is fun! We've even done some crazy things on our dates, like walking in the rain or dancing in the aisle of a supermarket to the music over the speaker system!*

- *Dating revolutionized our marriage. Several years ago when I was in medical school, our marriage was floundering, and we were totally stressed out. Twenty-hour workdays didn't help. We were becoming strangers and were well aware of the divorce statistics in the medical community. We knew we needed to do something to reignite our relationship. About that time we found your book. Having ten consecutive dates started a habit, and years later we are still dating.*

These couples learned the importance of date nights, and their stories show that dating can build your relationship and strengthen your marriage. In the digital world in which we live, more than ever couples need to connect with each other by having great dates, so we now offer you this updated edition of *10 Great Dates*.

Why This Update?

When we first published this book, the digital age was just beginning to take off. We had email and mobile phones, but social media and smartphones hadn't yet become the norm. Life was still busy and often stressful, but in recent years technology has complicated our busyness even while it's made some aspects of life easier and more convenient. For example, the digital revolution has virtually eliminated what we used to call "down time." We no longer have clear boundaries between personal time and work, school, or other commitments. With tools like Facebook, Twitter, Instagram, Snapchat, and Pinterest (just to name a few), we have the ability to be connected everywhere, to everyone, all the time. We occupy every in-between moment with screen time and rarely take time to just "be," to think and reflect, or to simply enjoy being with someone without distractions. If we aren't careful, social media and technology can rob us of the connections that mean the most to us even as they promise to connect us more than ever.

But don't panic! Even the challenges of technology and social media are no match for an intentional relationship. Based on current research and our work with couples over the years, we have crafted ten dates, each with marriage-enriching insights that will help you rid your relationship of distractions and infuse your marriage with new vitality and energy. And the payoff is huge! The latest research finds that couples who devote time specifically to one another at least once a week are markedly more likely to enjoy high-quality relationships and lower divorce rates, compared to couples who do not devote much couple time to one another.

Each date in Part 1 focuses on a skill you can use to develop a growing relationship. The first three dates focus on skills to develop your marriage coping system. Being committed to grow and to change together requires good communication skills as well as skills to process anger and resolve conflict in a positive way. Other dates help you encourage each other, develop a solid partnership based on individual strengths, and upgrade your love life. You will be challenged to work together and share responsibilities, to enrich your marriage while parenting your children, and to develop spiritual intimacy. Then you'll learn how to put all these skills together into an intentional marriage. Every chapter includes encouraging tips and experiences from actual dating couples. As you experience your own dates, you can energize your relationship—and have fun in the process!

In Part 2 we've provided a personal dating guide that syncs up with Part 1. Read the chapter in Part 1 and then use the appropriate section of the dating guide to put what you learn into practice. If you're not sure where to go or what to do, don't worry! We've included creative suggestions—both from us and from other dating couples—to help you keep the momentum going.

How to Maximize Your Dating Experience

Read the appropriate chapter before each date. If one of you doesn't have time to read the entire chapter, you can still get an overview by reading the chapter summary in the dating guide (Part 2). In the dating guide you'll also find duplicate, tear-out exercises with conversation starters for each date that will help you prepare for your dates and focus on improving your relationship.

Then date your spouse! In a relaxed setting (preferably away from interruptions and electronic devices), enjoy the opportunity to talk, to connect, and to fine-tune specific skills to enhance your marriage. The practical application during each date will make the difference, so don't skip it. Your ten great dates really can be fun— and they really will make a positive difference in your marriage. The promise of this book is that you *can* have a five-star marriage, and that these ten dates will help you achieve it. If you already have a five-star marriage, these dates will help you keep your marriage bright, alive, and strong.

What's required is a commitment to act on what you read. Your involvement makes the difference between merely reading a book and enriching your marriage. Statistics suggest it takes three weeks to break an old habit or start a new habit and an additional six weeks to feel good about it. We suggest ten dates to grow in emotional and physical intimacy, to improve your relationship, and to connect on a deeper level. Plus, we hope that dating will become a new habit that will benefit your marriage long after you've finished this book.

Don't Wait. Start Now!

Brian called to tell us that Megan, his thirty-six-year-old wife, had suffered a stroke. She was in intensive care with a blood clot on her brain and it was uncertain if she would live or die. Although we had never met, Brian asked if we might come to the hospital to visit Megan.

Brian explained that two weekends previously his parents had kept their five children so he and Megan could have a weekend getaway. During their weekend they experienced all ten dates! As a result, they reconnected, picked up some better ways to communicate, and had a fun getaway together. Neither would have dreamed that two weeks later Megan would have a massive stroke. When Megan was just beginning to recover, the first thing she said was,

"Call Arps.... say thanks.... *10 Great Dates.*" So Brian thought a visit from us might encourage her.

When we arrived at the intensive care unit, Brian told us that because of their weekend together he was now able to express his deep feelings to Megan, to pray with her, and to feel better equipped for what they were facing. Megan looked up at us and said simply, "fun" and "thank you." Together, they are traveling the long road to Megan's recovery while simultaneously building a stronger and deeper connection with each other.

While we hope you never have to face a life-threatening crisis like Megan and Brian faced, challenging times come to all of us. Don't miss this opportunity to strengthen your relationship now, and if a crisis does strike you will be prepared to face it together. You can prepare now by having *10 Great Dates*. The following steps will help you begin your dating experience on a positive note:

1. *Commit to ten dates.* Plan dates around something you enjoy doing and that allows for conversation. Put the dates on your calendar and make any necessary arrangements for childcare. (Do not take your kids with you on your dates!)

2. *Keep your commitment—even when the unexpected happens.* Sometimes children get sick and problems arise. When this happens, reschedule your date for the same week, if possible. Creating and maintaining momentum is important because each date builds on the one before.

3. *Cultivate a sense of anticipation.* Half the fun of having plans is eagerly anticipating them. Find ways to let your partner know you're looking forward to your date. Send texts and leave voice messages affirming you can't wait for your time together.

4. *Prepare.* Before your date, read the chapter and highlight anything you want to discuss. If you both complete the brief dating exercise before the date, you'll have more time to focus on conversation. But if not, you can complete the exercise during the date and then talk.

5. *Follow the guide for each date.* Don't use date time to deal with other relational issues. Focus on the topic of the date.

6. *Hold hands.* It's hard to fight or be negative when you're holding hands.

7. *Get started!* The key to building a strong and growing marriage is taking the time to invest in and work on the relationship.

Make a Commitment

The ten dates will only make a difference if you experience them. That's why we designed these dates to be simple, practical, interactive, inexpensive, and fun. So go on and make a commitment to have your *10 Great Dates.* (If it helps you to have it in writing, complete the form below.)

You'll be glad you took the time to connect with and encourage each other. Remember, yesterday is past and tomorrow isn't guaranteed. Today is the only gift of time you've been given. That's why it is called "the present." So give each other the present of *10 Great Dates!*

Our Dating Commitment

I agree to invest time in building our marriage by experiencing *10 Great Dates.*

Husband _____

Wife_____

Date_____

Part One

10 GREAT DATES

Choosing a High-Priority
MARRIAGE

Why do we do this to ourselves?" I (Claudia) asked in exasperation. "No one plans a tire blowout," Dave responded as he pulled the car to the side of the road. His logic was no comfort to me. I was way past the point of being objective or logical.

As we sat in our disabled car, we both felt frustrated and overwhelmed. *How could this be happening?* We were already exhausted after leading two back-to-back seminars. *Didn't we say we weren't doing that anymore?* And the night before had only increased our stress level. After eight hours in the car, we spent the evening trying to encourage friends who were struggling with problems related to their fifteen-year-old daughter.

Now we were stranded by the side of the road just as we were finally on our way to a one-week vacation in the mountains. The timing could not have been worse. The night air was frigid, our compact rental car was loaded down with luggage and food, and there we sat! We were too tired to unload the car to search for a spare tire, so we drove on to a hotel with a flat tire. The next morning, Dave replaced the tire and we were soon underway again.

But our difficulties didn't end there. Although we finally made it to our mountain cabin, soon after we arrived I noticed my back was becoming more and more uncomfortable. I tried walking it off, but the pain only increased. We spent the whole week doing nothing because I literally couldn't move. So much for our relaxing week of great hikes or a Great Date Getaway. It was just not going to happen!

Marriage sometimes resembles that blowout experience. We travel overloaded and stressed out. We keep talking about finding time to regroup and relax, but before we reach that point we have a blowout. Or, if you haven't experienced a major blowout in your relationship, perhaps you know what it's like to have a slow leak.

Whether a blowout or slow leak, the impact of stress can be toxic and the effects can spill over and affect not just our emotional and physical well-being, but also our relationships. Plus, chronic stress is both toxic and contagious. Think of a time you were in a bad mood, and before you knew it both of you were on a downward spiral. It happens to all of us.

Our Marriage Crisis

Years ago we came to a critical point in our marriage when we moved to Germany for Dave's job as a consultant for an international organization. It was a stressful move from the beginning. For starters, Dave was enthusiastic about the move, but Claudia was not. She missed home, family, and friends. We had three small children and no babysitters or "Mom's Day Out" opportunities. We didn't yet speak German and had no telephone for eight months. (This was way before mobile phones, instant messaging, FaceTime, Snapchat, and Skype.) Imagine being "offline" for several months! Today it's hard to go just a few hours without checking messages.

The one thing we did have was time together. But while we were physically together, emotionally we felt miles apart. Before moving to Germany, we had prided ourselves on having a great marriage. But over the years we'd allowed the busyness and demands of life to crowd out the time we spent together. Now that we were far from home and suddenly had nothing to do and no one to turn to but each other, we could no longer ignore the issues lurking beneath the surface. One morning as we stared at each other over coffee, we realized how far apart we had drifted.

"Dave, I don't feel like I even know you anymore," Claudia said, bursting into tears. "I don't feel comfortable here. I can't speak German. Our boys have no friends. Whatever happened to *us*? Now that we actually have time to talk to each other, what do we have to say?"

"Claudia, I know the stress and pressures of moving a family of five halfway across the world in six weeks have taken their toll," Dave replied, "but I also know we love each other. We can work things out."

The one thing we agreed on that morning was our need to regroup. We loved each other and were committed to our marriage, but the challenges of recent months had pushed us even further apart instead of pulling us together. We both wanted to renew our relationship and move closer to each other.

That Saturday morning we agreed to make a new start. We began to talk about our relationship and to focus on positive memories. Our conversation drifted back to when we met. We talked about what had attracted us to each other—Dave's easygoing personality and listening ear, Claudia's endless ideas and energy. (Somehow, after marriage, we had redefined those attractions as deficits—Dave was too slow and Claudia was overcommitted and lacked focus.)

As we talked about our first date, and how after just a few weeks of dating we felt a growing certainty that we had found in each other the one we wanted to do life with. By retracing our relationship to the dates that brought us together, we not only enjoyed reliving positive experiences from the past, we also found a tool to help us tackle the problems of the present. As we took a good look at our marriage—where it appeared to be heading and where we wanted it to go instead—we identified three marriage goals:

1. *We will evaluate where our marriage is now.* In thinking back over our history, we realized we felt most disconnected when we were overly busy and chronically stressed. We used to kid about having a front-door relationship—as one of us came in the door, the other handed off the kids and walked out the door. As we evaluated our marriage, we realized both of us were overcommitted and over-involved with our jobs and activities outside the home. We kept saying we needed to find time to talk through our issues, but we had difficulty actually making that time—until we moved to Germany. Then we didn't know what to do with it. We needed to focus by identifying exactly where our marriage was at so we could begin taking it in a new direction.

2. *We will set short- and long-term goals for our marriage.* We decided to look at where we wanted our marriage to be in six months, one year, five years, and even twenty-five years or more. When you have a future vision for your marriage, it's easier to make changes in the present to help you get there.

   We set some bite-sized goals and started to work toward each one step by step. Each achieved goal encouraged us to continue on to the next. Once a week we tried to put the boys to bed early so we could have a quiet, candlelit dinner for two. Sometimes we were just too tired to talk, but other times our late dinners were a catalyst for intimate conversations and sharing. And as difficult as it was to find childcare, we began to schedule monthly dates.

3. *We will learn new skills—or relearn to use the old ones we've stopped practicing.* There were basic relationship skills we already knew but no longer used, such as really listening to each other (rather than anticipating what we wanted to say when the other person stopped talking). We also worked on dealing with anger and conflict. It was hard not to repeat old patterns of attacking each other, but when we took time to calm down and tried resolving issues together, our relationship was strengthened. Often the problem wasn't knowing what to do, but doing what we knew!

Setting goals really helped us turn around. We were able to reaffirm that we had a great partnership, but it took lots of work and it didn't happen overnight. We discovered marriage is a journey—not a destination—and today we still work to make our marriage a high priority. Consider the following three principles that can energize your marriage and keep it a high priority.

Three Principles for a High-Priority Marriage

In our national survey of long-term marriages, we found three common strands in marriages that are healthy and growing. In a healthy long-term marriage, both spouses:

- Put their marriage first.
- Commit to growing together.

- Work at staying close.

Let's consider how each of these three principles can help you to develop a high-priority marriage.

PUT YOUR MARRIAGE FIRST

When we marry, we promise to stand by each other in sickness and in health till death do us part. It's a commitment of choosing and preferring each other above all others. Here's another way of looking at it. If you put anything—your career, children, community and church involvement, sports, hobbies, screens, or whatever—before your commitment to your partner, nothing you can say, buy, give, or promise your spouse will really satisfy.

Is there anything in your life right now that you prioritize over your relationship with your spouse? What about your job? Do you really have to work twelve-hour days to survive? Or do you tend to put your children first? We know, your spouse is an adult and can wait, but consider this: *Your children will wait while you invest some moments to prioritize your marriage, but your marriage is not going to wait until your children grow up.* One of the greatest gifts you can give your children is a strong and healthy relationship with your spouse. Bottom line: Unless you are willing to make the relationship with your spouse a higher priority than other relationships and activities, you will not have a growing marriage.

Most would probably agree that the marriage relationship should be a top priority, but in days, hours, and minutes, sometimes it just doesn't work out that way—even when we try. Matt and Kendra have three boys under age four. Sometimes the stress of parenting gets to them. "We really try to make our relationship a priority," Kendra said. "Last week I went through the hassle of getting a sitter and we slipped away to a restaurant, but we just sat there and stared at each other. We were too exhausted even to talk!"

Love in marriage is a delicate balancing act. Some things we can control; others we have to juggle. On that evening maybe Kendra and Matt should have gone home and curled up in bed with a book or watched a movie instead of forcing tired conversation over a meal.

What's your situation? Are you also time and energy challenged? What needs to take a lower priority so you can put your marriage first? For instance, in mapping out your schedule for the next several weeks, why not book date times before other commitments? Schedule other commitments in the time you have left. When it comes to prioritizing marriage, such small choices and decisions may not seem very important, but they all add up. No matter how small the decision, make marriage your first priority.

A Practical Tip for Putting Your Marriage First

You can be proactive in prioritizing your marriage even while dealing with daily stresses. For example, you can begin to de-stress even before you get home. Devote time on your way home from work to thinking positive thoughts about your partner. Allow your thoughts to dwell on a couple times when you felt really close to your spouse. Then when you get home, hug your spouse for twenty seconds. According to brain neurochemistry research, when you hug for at least twenty seconds you release oxytocin and endorphins into the blood stream, which decreases cortisol and other stress hormones, and that's why the twenty-second hug will help you de-stress!

COMMIT TO GROW TOGETHER

Building a high-priority marriage requires a lifelong commitment to grow and change together. Every marriage has problems. The difference between those that make it and those that don't is that the successful ones are committed to growing together and working to solve the problems that arise.

A commitment to growth goes beyond just sticking together. It's also a commitment to adapt to each other's changing needs. Jessica confided, "Jackson and I have been married for only six years, yet we both have changed so much. If we change as much in the next six years, I'm afraid we'll grow apart. How can we make it over the long haul?"

Our response to Jessica's question was to affirm that building a vibrant, long-term marriage requires a willingness to grow and adapt to each other's changing needs. We don't have to fear these changes. We just need to make it a habit to adjust continually to maintain the same loving, alive relationship.

This is especially true for new parents. Lauren, who has an almost-one-year-old baby girl put it this way: "I've found that as a new mom, just when I think I've figure it out, things change again. Over the past eleven months as a new mother, I have been caught off guard by how often my baby changes. As soon as I have a sleeping and eating schedule down, she throws me a curve ball and we start all over! It's a never-ending challenge, but I am getting better at it."

It can be the same in marriage. We will never get to a point where we can say, "There! We have a great relationship so now we can stop trying." Marriage is always a work in progress.

If we refuse to grow and change, we will only have a mediocre marriage. Adapting to each other requires self-sacrifice. It means being each other's best friend—that one person the other can always count on.

What have you done lately to adapt to each other, to grow and change in response to each other? Do you share common interests? While you benefit from your differences, you also benefit from shared experiences. As you go through your ten dates, you will have opportunities to talk about things you would like to do together to build your friendship and to keep on understanding, adapting, and growing together.

WORK AT STAYING CLOSE

In a high-priority marriage, not only do partners grow and adapt to each other, they also work at staying close. Unfortunately, many things tend to push us apart—like overcommitment or too much time using social media or surfing the internet, which both can lead to lack of sleep. To combat the things that push us apart, we try to avoid negative situations as much as possible. For instance, when we find ourselves overcommitted once again, we try to pace ourselves and say "no" when we need to. When you have a choice to make, ask yourself, *Will this action or attitude bring us closer together, or will it put distance in our relationship?*

Working at staying close will help you build an intimate love relationship.

In a healthy, growing marriage, partners complement each other and experience a unique oneness with each other through physical and emotional intimacy (and of course, dating!). They enjoy each other and are committed to building their friendship. They stay close through focusing on helping each other. Any help we offer our spouse helps our marriage partnership. Any pain, hurt, insult, any lack of support or faithfulness, any failure to help our spouse will negatively impact our marriage.

You can be the most positive, reinforcing person in your partner's life if you are willing to follow these three principles of putting your marriage first, committing to growing together, and working at staying close.

Note from a Dating Couple

Our first great date reminded us of some wonderful times we've shared and motivated us to start doing some of those things again. We smiled and talked a lot. Looking forward to Date Two!

Time To Prioritize Your Marriage!

Now it's time for you to affirm that your marriage is a high priority. On this date you will take a trip down memory lane and together remember when you first met and how you couldn't bear to be apart. What attracted you to each other? If you met online, what was your impression when you met in person? Focusing on good memories can remind you of how important your marriage is, and reliving your love story can reignite the spark in your relationship. You will also look at your marriage, affirm what is great about it, and consider how to make your relationship even better as you experience your own *10 Great Dates*. And remember to try a twenty-second hug!

*Turn to Date One in the Dating Guide and get
ready to have a high-priority marriage!*

Learning to
COMMUNICATE

Instant communication has upsides and downsides. Some couples use technology to deepen their sense of connection when apart. Here's how one wife describes the upside, "My husband and I feel closer now that we text while he's at work. All it takes is a quick 'I love you!' 'I miss you!' or 'Looking forward to tonight.' Or sometimes we send pictures of what we're doing throughout the day."

On the other hand, communicating through technology can also be a barrier to intimacy and couple closeness. Here is how one wife describes the downside. "I just hate it when we're in the middle of a conversation and my husband looks down to read a message he just received." Definitely, not a marriage builder.

When it comes to technology and communication within a marriage, the important thing is not to eliminate technology but to keep it from replacing time spent talking to one another directly, ideally face-to-face.

What about you? How do you typically communicate with your spouse? Text? Phone? Email? FaceTime? Are you more likely to check social media to see what your partner is up to rather than having a conversation to find out?

One survey found that the average couple spends just 34 minutes together each day (excluding sleep time). We wonder how much of that 34 minutes is spent talking instead of in silence in front of a screen.[1] Certainly none of us took a vow of silence after marriage, so why do we apparently stop talking to each other?

Ryan and Aubrey wondered too. At a Marriage Alive seminar, Ryan said in frustration, "I can talk to my dog but not to my wife. I always know how my dog is going to respond. Aubrey is a different story. I never know how she will react."

"Ryan pats the dog and walks right by me," Aubrey said. "I feel closed out of his life; I feel invisible—like he doesn't even see me."

Three Styles of Communication

If Ryan and Aubrey are going to connect, they need to learn how to communicate effectively with each other. A relationship is only as intimate as the conversations you have with each other. Words can help to build your relationship, or they can destroy the very foundations of your marriage. It's your choice. By understanding three styles of communication, you can hone your communication skills and develop the habit of using the more helpful ones.

STYLE ONE: CHATTERING

Chattering refers to surface conversations. "Did you sleep well?" "Have you seen the remote?" "Better take an umbrella today. Looks like rain." "I can't find my car keys." "Have you seen my phone?" Chattering is part of healthy conversation; we use it every day. But problems inevitably arise when chatter becomes the predominant communication pattern. Chattering is safe—no sparks fly—but if that is as deep as your communication goes, it will render your relationship shallow and lonely.

STYLE TWO: CONFRONTING

Our mentors and dear friends, Drs. David and Vera Mace, refer to confronting as the style of communication with the sting in the tail. It hurts! In this style, we make "you" statements like:

"You just don't listen when I try to talk to you."

"You make me so angry when you're late and don't text or call."

"Why" questions like:

"Why did you do that?"

"Why can't you think before you speak?"

"Why can't you remember to hang up your coat when you come in?"

When we use "you" statements and "why" questions, we're choosing to attack the other person, often without even realizing what we're doing. Confronting might also include using absolute words like "always" and "never."

"You always think you're right!"

"You always have to have things your way."

"You never listen to me!"

"You never want to know my thoughts about anything!"

Confronting might also take the form of sarcasm or comparing:

"Well, aren't you just Miss Perfect?"

"Why can't you be more like...?"

When confronting becomes a pattern, we've got trouble. Our goal whenever we get into this mode (and at times we all do) is to get out of it as quickly as we can! We needed a way to throw a red flag when our communication turns negative, so we came up with a cue. We simply say, "Ouch, I feel a pinch!" It's an easy way to let the other know we feel attacked, whether or not it was intentional. Use our cue or come up with what will work for you as a way to alert each other that you want to move on to a more helpful communication style. A wise partner will acknowledge the red flag and step back.

We sometimes still fall into a confronting style, but at least our attacks are mostly unintentional slips. We try to follow two simple principles:

1. We will not intentionally attack each other.
2. We will not defend ourselves.

On those occasions when we do slip, the one who feels attacked can diffuse the confrontation by resisting the temptation to justify or be defensive. Our agreement helps us move on and connect more positively.

While all couples slip into the confronting style from time to time, healthy couples use them less often. And when you do mess up and one of you throws a red flag, you can use a repair tactic that deescalates negative communication to set things right. Examples of repair tactics include apologizing, using humor, taking a break to calm down, and so on. Then you can move on to the more helpful communication style—connecting.

Note from a Dating Couple

One of our favorite tactics when we get in the confronting pattern is to stop and ask, "Is it my day to be right or is it yours?" That's usually enough to stop the escalation and realize, "Hey, we're on the same team here. You can be right today and I'll be right tomorrow."

(In the next chapter we talk about using this tactic personally.)

STYLE THREE: CONNECTING

The connecting style of communication is the meat-and-potatoes style for all who want to build a strong and healthy relationship. If we really want to connect, we need to be willing to make ourselves vulnerable by sharing what's going on inside. Our agreement not to attack each other or to defend ourselves creates a safe place for us to share our true feelings. We trust the other to resist defending, justifying, or attacking, and to handle our feelings with tenderness when we make ourselves vulnerable. This opens the door for truly intimate conversations.

Sharing feelings on a deeper level helps build a strong communication system that helps us to handle problems. When two people really connect both their brains and their hearts and can understand the "why" behind the other's viewpoint, they are much more likely to manage their problems well. Plus, sharing feelings with one another has physical benefits—your body releases oxytocin, a hormone that counteracts the effects of stress and helps to strengthen the emotional bond we feel for one another.[2]

For connecting conversation to be effective, we have to focus on being fully present and available to one another. That begins with basics like being willing to turn off the TV, close the laptop, and set aside any other electronic devices. Making an effort to be emotionally present—by listening attentively and seeking to understand one another—results in significant deposits in the relationship bank account.

We use all three styles of communication. Chattering is just a part of our daily conversations, and from time to time we slip into the confronting style. No one has perfect communication—at least we don't—but the key is to log more time using the connecting style. Listen to your conversations for the next day or so and try to identify which communication styles you tend to use the most. And if you find you need more help in using the connecting style, just keep reading. You can learn to connect through sharing your deeper emotions with each other.

How to Express Feelings

For many years we've used a simple formula to express our feelings to each other, our children, and others.[3] It is clear, simple, and nonthreatening when used with the right attitude at the right time. It includes two simple statements: "Let me tell you how I feel" and "Now tell me how you feel."

"Let me tell you how I feel. I feel . . ." State how you feel clearly, directly, and lovingly by completing this statement, "Let me tell you how I feel. I feel. . . . " For example, "I feel . . . frustrated," or angry, alone, hurt, disappointed, anxious, happy, joyful, and so forth. Express your feelings by focusing on "I" statements and avoid attacking the other person.

Don't confuse "I *feel*" with "I *think*." If you can substitute "think" for "feel," then it is not a feeling. For instance, "I *feel* that you hurt me!" expresses a thought and judgment. It is the confronting/attacking style of communication in the disguise of a feeling statement. A true feeling statement would be to say, "I feel hurt when my opinion doesn't seem to count." You can also state your feelings by using the words; "I am," as in "I am hurt when my opinion is ignored."

Focus your statements on expressing what you feel inside and not on attacking or blaming your spouse. Feelings are neither right nor wrong; they simply are—and it's valuable to know how your mate feels. This leads to the second part of the feelings formula.

"Now tell me how you feel." After you have clearly and lovingly stated how you feel, say, "Now tell me how you feel." Then be prepared to listen. Don't judge or criticize feelings. Remember, they are neither right nor wrong! Remind yourself that your partner's feelings come from their perspective and their perspective is their reality.

We were teaching this concept in a seminar when a participant interrupted, "Wait a minute. How can you say feelings are neither right nor wrong? Some feelings are just plain sinful!"

A great discussion followed on the differences between how we feel and how we act, and about what distinguishes a thought from a true feeling. For example, someone might try to use feeling statements to get off the hook easily by saying something like, "I don't feel like going to work today, "I don't feel like being a thoughtful spouse," or "I feel like having an affair."

"We may feel a certain way," another seminar participant said, "but that's not an excuse for doing or not doing what is right. I wouldn't have my job very long if I told my boss, 'I don't feel like going to work today.'"

"I agree," said another, "but maybe the statement 'I don't feel like going to work' is not the real feeling or issue. Maybe you actually do feel worn out, taken advantage of, or bored with the job."

"Or," still another added, "maybe the statement 'I feel like having an affair' is really saying on a deeper level, 'I'm bored with my marriage; I feel disconnected from my spouse; I want more romance and excitement.'"

Now we were getting down to the real feelings. Feelings are fragile, and we must handle them with care. But if we can get to the real issue through sharing our feelings, we can attack the problem instead of each other, and at the same time strengthen our relationship.

It was at this point that one seminar participant exclaimed, "It's just too hard! I've been 'me' for forty years, and I'm not going to change now. Besides, all this feeling stuff seems fake and unnatural to me." Maybe you feel this way, too.

We understand. Learning to express our feelings wasn't easy for us either. Clear communication is hard work! It's hard to let the other know how you really feel. How will he or she use that information? When we first tried to express our true feelings, it was easier for me (Claudia) than for Dave. When I said how I felt, Dave would counter with, "Why do you feel that way?" or "No one in their right mind should feel that way!" He had to learn not to judge my feelings—feelings are neither right nor wrong—but it was good information for him to know how I felt. I wasn't looking for agreement, just empathy. Empathy becomes easier when you realize it doesn't necessarily mean you agree; it just means you are trying to understand the issue from your spouse's perspective.

The couples in the seminar were beginning to understand when a participant named Jeff said, "This all sounds great, but I couldn't say how I felt if I wanted to—I just don't have the words! My dad said only three words most of the time I was growing up, and none of them had anything to do with how he felt—and me, well, I'm a chip off the old block."

To help Jeff venture into the world of feelings, we brainstormed words we could use to express our feelings when we don't know what to say. If you have difficulty expressing feelings, maybe our list will help you get started.

I feel ...

hurt	angry	frustrated
happy	threatened	lonely
confused	inspired	stressed
loved	depressed	used
excited	anxious	joyful
peaceful	attacked	energetic
irritated	sad	helpless
content	responsible	belittled
overwhelmed	encouraged	remorseful
left out	broken	sick
afraid	trapped	stifled
squelched	tense	betrayed
nervous	silly	pressured

grateful	abused	scared
perplexed	misunderstood	alone
satisfied	optimistic	pessimistic
crushed	numb	bored
discouraged	ignored	pleased
uneasy	deprived	embarrassed
relaxed	upset	dissatisfied
guilty	useless	resentful
rejected	concerned	tired
foolish	annoyed	excited
calm	relieved	playful
nervous	devastated	jealous
humiliated	vulnerable	hopeful

How comfortable are you with words like these? Are you willing to try the feelings formula? Are there feelings you hesitate to talk about with your spouse? If so, it may help first to write down how you feel. Use what you write as the foundation for telling your partner how you feel (or let your spouse read what you wrote), and ask for his or her feelings in response. Then try to understand how your spouse feels.

For example, you might be concerned that you are both overusing your credit cards and finding it too convenient and easy to shop online. You fear that financial troubles are in your future and want to talk about it and find a solution now. Remember, overspending is the problem you want to attack. You could write something like, "I'm concerned that we're spending too much online and are about to max out our credit cards." However you word it, *attack the problem, not each other*! And remember to listen in response.

Listen for the Total Message

Why is it so hard to listen? Could it be that instead of really listening we are already thinking ahead and strategizing about what we want to say? Listening is more than politely waiting for your turn to talk. Listening is worth the effort! Many conflicts begin as misunderstandings. If we would just take the time to listen and understand, we would save ourselves much time and misery.

For years we had a card on our refrigerator door that read, "Listen, don't react!" But at times we still reverse it—we react and don't listen! Remember the old adage not to criticize the other person until you've walked a mile in their shoes? Stop and imagine you are the one experiencing the feelings your partner is describing. Not only do we need to practice empathizing with the other person, but we need to understand the total message the other person is communicating because that message includes much more than the spoken words.

A few years ago, a major corporation did a study to determine what makes up the "total message" in communication.[4] Here are three things they discovered.

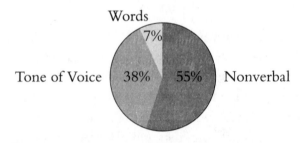

Words
7%
Tone of Voice   38%   55%   Nonverbal

1. Nonverbal communication accounts for 55 percent of the total message. This includes things like shrugs, stares, and glares. (We all know "the look"!) Picture one partner trying to talk while the other's attention is glued to a screen. Have you ever agreed with your mate verbally but given another message with a look of resentment on your face? There is no colder place to be than with a spouse who is using the "right" words to gloss over bitterness, anger, and hostility (like saying, "Sorry," but not really meaning it).

2. Tone of voice accounts for 38 percent of the total message. This includes the sighs and nagging tones that creep into our conversations. Have you ever said, "Okay," when it really wasn't okay? Your tone of voice can send a completely different message than the words you speak.

This is so hard because it can be difficult to hear our own tone of voice or see the expression on our face. One clue your nonverbals or tone of voice is sending a different message than your words is if your spouse acts defensively.

3. Spoken words make up only 7 percent of the total message. The next time you say something, know that your words are only a very small part of the message you're communicating.

This research simply affirms what most of us already know—it is vitally important to really listen to each other. And that includes "listening" to nonverbals and tone of voice as well as words. For the average woman, emotional intimacy is nurtured not just by talking but by feeling that the listener is tuned in and attempting to understand. And here's a plus. When a woman's emotional intimacy levels go up, her desire for physical intimacy goes up.

The reverse is true for men—as physical intimacy goes up, their desire for emotional intimacy goes up. It is also easier for men to communicate when their bodies are active. So going on daily walks together is good not only for your body, but also for your relationship—you can talk while you walk and get twice the benefits. Or give each other a big hug as you're walking out the door—research also shows that cuddling first diminishes the likelihood of triggering a negative physiological response in men when the topic of conversation might otherwise cause a reaction. And as you cuddle, here's a tip for the guys: you don't have to solve all the problems your wife talks about, you just need to listen. Seeking to understand does not mean you are agreeing with your spouse. And later, when you do come to the point of seeking a solution, you may find that instead of playing tug of war you can each take a step toward each other and meet in the middle.

The Strawberry Patch

As marriage educators, you'd think we might have this communication stuff all figured out, but there are still times we get it wrong. At times we slip into the confronting mode. Other times we fail to listen to each other well. Our marriage is still a work in progress. In fact, we remember one day when we used all three styles of communication.

It was a beautiful Saturday morning. At breakfast Dave announced he was going to spend the day working in the yard. This was not his favorite activity so, as we discussed the day ahead, we did some chattering. I (Claudia) did not want to distract the gardener from his tasks, so I spent the day at my desk working on a writing project. Since we were both being so productive, we felt good about our plans for the day. Later that afternoon, Dave dragged into the house—dirty, tired, sore muscles and all—but he had "done the yard!" and wanted to show off his accomplishments. So together we went outside to take a yard tour.

Everything was transformed! Grass mowed. Plants pruned. Flowerbeds weeded and mulched. I was thrilled—until I came around the house to my strawberry patch. This was the year the strawberries were really going to produce, and I could already envision strawberries on ice cream, strawberries on cereal, and strawberries on shortcake!

As I looked at what was supposed to be my strawberry patch, I exploded with confrontation. "What have you done? Why did you do that?" Dave had inadvertently pulled up all the cultivated plants and left behind only the wild strawberry plants that needed to be removed!

"Dave, you've ruined my strawberries! How could you do that to me—after the hours of work I've put in! I can't believe you didn't at least ask me about what to pull!" My anger was vented, and Dave secretly wished he had just cemented in the whole yard the year before. Our confronting pattern was alive and well. How could we get out of this mess?

We knew we couldn't solve the problem until we calmed down. Both of us had said things we regretted and it was time for damage control. "Dave," I began, "I didn't mean to attack you. I just feel so disappointed that my strawberries are gone. I worked hard on them, and this is so frustrating to me!"

"I feel frustrated too," Dave responded. "I spent the whole day in the yard, my body hurts, I'm tired, and now I find out I did it wrong. It's just that the wild strawberries actually had little red berries on them. I assumed they were the real strawberries. I'm really sorry!"

Slowly, we were moving into the connecting style of communication. About that time, we eyed the strawberry victims. The cultured plants were in a heap in the driveway. They were the problem we needed to address, so we began to focus on them. As we began to think creatively together, we decided to replant them. Clearing out the wild plants gave us more room to replant the real strawberries. My strawberries were replanted before dark, and our relationship was restored. Plus, the strawberries lived! And we did have strawberries on ice cream, strawberries on cereal, and strawberries short-cake—and even chocolate-covered strawberries in our bedroom!

It takes determination, effort, and courage to develop the skill of connecting with each other in positive communication. But take it from us, it's worth all the effort! In the next chapter you will see how developing the connecting communication pattern can help you manage and solve problems together as a couple.

Now, turn to Date Two in the Dating Guide and get ready to listen, to talk, and to have some fun. (And remember to turn off your electronics!)

_____

Solving Problems as a
COUPLE

Did you know that over 250 million roses are produced each year for Valentine's Day? It's an astounding number, but what says "I love you" more than a dozen red roses? While roses remind us of love and marriage, you may also have heard the saying, "Marriage is not a bed of roses." Actually, in some ways it is, but with every rose comes thorns of conflict and disagreement. Some thorns are easy to deal with but others are harder to clip and need to be managed in a way that doesn't cause constant pain.

Before marriage, we tend to see each other through rose-colored glasses. After marriage, it doesn't take long to discover that dealing with thorns is an ongoing task. As much as we would have liked to have the beauty without the beast, it's unrealistic to assume we can have roses without thorns.

John Gottman, PhD, a marital researcher at the University of Washington, has conducted impressive research on the ongoing problems married couples face. His findings helped us understand that some of the thorny issues we deal with are perpetual issues with no once-and-for-all solution. His research revealed that 69 percent of the issues couples disagree about are of the perpetual variety — they aren't going to be entirely solved or go away. Instead, couples needed to learn how to manage them so that the thorns weren't continually pricking them.[1]

Fortunately, we can learn how to manage conflict and process anger. Let's begin by looking at how you presently handle conflict.

How Do You Handle Conflict?

Let's take a trip to the zoo. The ways we handle conflict can be compared to certain animal characteristics. Do you identify with any of the following?[2]

THE TURTLE: "I WITHDRAW"

I (Dave) am a turtle. When faced with conflict, my tendency is to withdraw. I pull my head inside my shell for the duration. Claudia, who occasionally likes an argument, can beat on my shell, but to no avail. I won't come out until the storm passes.

Are you a turtle? Do you tend to withdraw from conflict? You may withdraw physically, like getting up and walking out of the room, or you may withdraw emotionally by tuning out the other person. Perhaps you feel hopeless and defeated before you even begin to address the issue, so why discuss it? Here's why: withdrawing hurts the relationship and prevents you from finding a way to manage or solve the problem. Take the risk to poke your head out and share what's going on beneath that self-protective shell.

THE SKUNK: "I ATTACK"

I (Claudia) hate to admit it, but I can be a skunk. When I feel attacked or misunderstood, my natural tendency is to spray Dave and make him stink. I would rather focus on what he did or didn't do to avoid any responsibility for my part.

Do you identify with the skunk? Do you spray noxious fumes on your spouse when your expectations aren't met or when you feel attacked? Many skunks are masters of sarcasm and insults. They use their quick verbal skills to make the other person look bad and to deflect attention from their own shortcomings. If you identity with the skunk, then it's important to utilize your verbal skills to share your feelings in a positive way using the connecting style we talked about in Date 2.

Over the years of working with couples, we've met many turtles who are married to skunks. We've even observed a new breed—the skurtle. The skurtle, a combination of the skunk and the turtle, handles conflict by attacking the other person and then withdrawing into his or her shell! Skurtles have a double challenge—coming out of their shell without attacking the other.

THE BEAVER: "I AVOID"

The beaver avoids conflict by just getting busy. Beavers easily immerse themselves in a project and spend long hours at work. They increase their hours volunteering for another community or church activity. Or they might disappear by spending hours online or interacting on social media. They do whatever it takes to evade conflict!

Joe is a beaver. When an emotional or heated issue comes up, instead of addressing it head on, he finds something else to do. He's uncomfortable with emotional talk and would rather do anything—even mow the lawn—than tackle a heated issue with his wife.

If you identify with Joe, here's a tip. While avoiding conflict may seem like the safest approach, it's not going to solve problems. Take the risk and share your deeper emotions with your spouse by using the connecting style of communication we talked about in the previous chapter.

THE CHAMELEON: "I YIELD"

Chameleons are pleasers—they change colors to blend into the environment as a means of avoiding conflict. They agree with whatever opinions are being expressed. When they are with a quiet group, they are quiet. When they are with a loud group, they become loud. Their desire to fit in prevents them from expressing their real opinions and feelings, so when conflict arises they'll go along with the crowd.

Not always, but often the chameleon is a wife (who may be married to a beaver) who abruptly leaves a marriage after several years of "giving in." No one can understand what triggered her sudden departure because no one had a clue she was unhappy—that's how good she was at blending in. But everyone has a limit—like a balloon that stretches and stretches and then suddenly pops.

Marriage therapist Michele Weiner-Davis has seen this so many times in her Divorce Busting work that she labels this phenomenon the "Walkaway Wife Syndrome."[3] Not every chameleon becomes a walkaway spouse, but being a constant pleaser and or adapter doesn't help to build a strong marriage. Lila is a chameleon. She grew up in a family with a domineering mother and three older sisters. The best way to get along with everyone was to keep her opinions to herself and blend in. She learned to be a pleaser, and when she married Chuck this pattern continued. Fortunately, Lila has learned to speak up and be more assertive.

Are you a chameleon? Do you like to blend in and keep your opinions to yourself? While you may want to avoid confrontations, you need to work at speaking up and becoming more assertive.

THE OWL: "I INTELLECTUALIZE"

Like turtles, owls avoid conflict, but they use different methods. Owls intellectualize. Their motto is, "Avoid messy feelings at all costs!" Owls gladly discuss an issue on an intellectual level but have no feelings from their cranium down. They deal with facts, facts, and nothing but the facts.

Mark is an owl. He's a hard worker and dependable, so he has a difficult time understanding when his wife forgets to pick up the cleaning, especially when he needs a clean shirt for a big meeting the next day. Do you identify with the owl? Then you can appreciate your ability to think things through and make wise decisions but you might need to give your partner, who may be more free-spirited, a little slack.

THE GORILLA: "I INTIMIDATE "

Gorillas have to win at all costs. Their favorite weapons are manipulation and intimidation. Underneath their tough skin they may be very insecure and want to look good no matter what the cost. They keep mental files of old grudges, hurts, and wrongs as weapons to use when they feel threatened. They power up by focusing on all the reasons you are wrong and all the reasons they are right! The gorilla's gruff exterior may hide a softer, gentler side, but you might not recognize it when the gorilla is angry!

We'll never forget the seminar where one participant was the classic gorilla. He constantly interrupted us to tell us what we were doing wrong and was quick to insult his wife. The solution came from among the participants. During a break, several husbands slipped away and came back with a huge bunch of bananas for our gorilla. He finally got the message.

Do you identify with the gorilla? How important is it to feel that you are right? Do you have a hard time letting go of past hurts and find yourself going through a litany of ways others have wronged you? If so, in chapter 9 we'll be talking about the importance of forgiveness and how to let go of old hurts

WHAT'S YOUR STYLE?

Do you identify with any of our animal friends? One couple in a seminar identified with us. Here's how the wife describes their experience.

Note from a Dating Couple

The descriptions of the turtle and skunk struck a chord with me because they describe my husband and me exactly. It was very helpful for us to discuss our tendencies and consider our own history. For example, my parents were both turtles and preferred to avoid conflict. It seemed to work for them because they figured out how to calm down on their own and get over things. They rarely argued. If they were frustrated, they never talked about it. I am so much like them. I hate confrontation so I'd rather just go in my shell and work it out on my own. On the other hand, my husband grew up in a home with parents who were both skunks. They duked it out all the time, but then they got over it. He is more that way. Understanding our animal styles gives us tools to communicate better and to compromise a bit more. Now when my husband is acting like a skunk, I might say, "I know you're upset right now, but let's talk about it after I go for a walk and cool down."

Just as this couple did, you too can benefit from understanding how you typically react to conflict. Then you can move forward by choosing a better approach to solving problems as a couple. Whether the issues in your marriage tend to be minor irritations (how to squeeze the toothpaste tube, the battle or the thermostat, or how to roll the toilet paper) or major concerns (finances, parenting styles, sex, in-laws, priorities), the key is to stop avoiding or attacking your spouse and instead try to look at your issues from the same side. In other words, rather than seeing each other as the opposition, position yourselves as a team in opposition to the conflict.

In *Fighting for Your Marriage*, authors and marital researchers Drs. Howard Markman, Scott Stanley, and Susan Blumberg write: "You have a choice when dealing with a problem. Either you will nurture a sense that you are working together against the problem, or you will operate as if you are working against each other."[4]

As we discussed in chapter 2, learning to express your feelings and seeking to understand your partner's feelings will facilitate good communication. But what happens when in the midst of trying to talk about an issue, one or both of you become angry with the other? Rather than reacting like the animals, you can choose to work at processing your anger as a team.

Understanding and Processing Anger

Two thousand years ago the apostle Paul had some good advice for the church at Ephesus: Don't sin when you're angry, and don't let the sun go down on your anger.[5] That's still good advice for us today, but how can we possibly do this? We've discovered two significant strategies that help us process anger positively—we identify the primary emotion and we make an anger contract.

IDENTIFY THE PRIMARY EMOTION

Did you realize anger is actually a secondary emotion? That means we feel it *after* feeling a primary emotion like *fear, frustration,* or *hurt.* For instance, consider the stormy night when Dave was late coming home and didn't text or call Claudia to let her know he was going to be late. When he didn't show up as expected, she was fearful he'd been in an accident. By the time he finally walked in the door, Claudia was no longer concerned about his safety; she was just very angry that he hadn't called. Or consider the husband who goes from feeling frustrated to angry when his wife spends hours on social media after the children are in bed even though it's supposed to be their time alone together. Or think of the wife who felt hurt because her husband said something that left her feeling devalued and unappreciated. Yes, his words hurt, but now she's angry.

Think back to the last time you were angry. Was your anger the result of fear? Were you frustrated about something to the point of becoming angry? Or were you hurt? Taking time to identify the primary emotions behind your anger will help you process it together. For instance, when Claudia was able to explain to Dave how frightened she had been when he was late, it was easier for both to understand her angry explosion. Acknowledging her fear—the primary emotion—helped her process and move through her anger so she could eventually give Dave a hug and say, "I'm so glad you are home safely. I was afraid you were in an accident!"

By understanding the root of your anger—that is your primary emotion—you can more easily determine the best way to process your anger and facilitate thoughtful action. So the next time you're feeling angry, pause for a moment and see if you can identify the primary emotion driving your anger.

MAKE AN ANGER CONTRACT

A helpful tool we learned years ago from our mentors, Drs. David and Vera Mace, has helped us to calm down and process our anger before it gets out of control. The Maces taught us how to make an anger contract. We actually signed a written contract with these three commitments:[6]

1. I will tell you when I am getting angry with you.
2. I will not vent my anger on you.
3. I will ask for your help in finding a solution for my anger.

Here's how our contract works. In our contract, we agree to tell each other when we realize we are getting angry. Otherwise, one of us could be angry and the other wouldn't know it! (Guess who that might be? *Not* Claudia!) We agree that we aren't going to lash out or attack the other but instead will ask for help in dealing with whatever is causing the anger. One caution: Make this contract with each other when you are not in the middle of dealing with an issue!

When we bring up our anger contract, we (at least one of us) may need to take a break to cool off. (One fast and effective method is to focus on your breathing. Count slowly to five as you take a long slow, deep breath in, and then count to five as you slowly exhale. Do this for at least five minutes.) Humor helps us, but not everyone responds well to humor when tensions are high. When we're in the middle of a tense discussion, sometimes one of us will say, "Whose day is it to be right? Mine or yours?" That's usually enough to produce a chuckle and release some tension. Whatever your strategy, the goal is to find a way to get on your spouse's team instead of competing against them.

Once the anger is diffused, then we can discuss the source of the conflict. But until we process the anger, we can't really manage the situation that is causing the anger. So we encourage you to make your own anger contract. This will make a huge difference when you get to the step of actually trying to find a solution. It is possible to share negative feelings in a positive way if you have made your own anger contract. It will help you not to attack each other or defend yourself.

Now that you have processed your anger and calmed down, you can address the issue at hand. First you need to clearly identify the issue that is causing the problem. This may actually be the toughest part of the process. Many arguments are not about the real issue.

Take Turns Talking

To help you define the issue, we suggest a simple exercise that will help you get on the same page. For this exercise, you're only *talking* about the problem or issue, not trying to resolve it. This process involves expressing negative feelings, and for that you need a structure. One suggested great tool is to use the speaker/listener technique as a way to "share the floor."[7]

As in parliamentary proceedings, the speaker has the floor. You can pick up a pen, your glasses, a book, a cup — anything — and say, "I have the floor." You are announcing that you want to use this tool to talk about the issue at hand. The person with the floor is the speaker. The person without the floor is the listener.

The goal is to discuss the issue, stay on topic, and get to the point where you both understand the other's feelings and viewpoints. Again, the goal is *not to solve the problem!* This exercise works because it separates defining the problem from trying to solve the problem. We suggest combining this exercise with the feelings formula from chapter 2 (page 34–37). Sharing the floor gives you the structure you need to do the hard work of talking about the issue and the feelings formula keeps you safe by avoiding attacking statements.

A Word of Caution for Guys from Dave

Guys naturally want to solve the problem. That's what we do, but first you need to discover what the real issue is before you can work together with your wife to find a solution.

Once someone takes the floor, they are the speaker. Then they can pass the pen back and forth so the listener becomes the speaker and so on. Here are the rules for the speaker and the listener:

Rules for speaker:

- Speak only for yourself. Don't engage in mindreading!
- Keep statements brief. Don't go on and on.
- Stop and let the listener paraphrase what you just said.

Rules for the listener:

- Paraphrase what you hear the speaker say.
- Focus on the speaker's total message, not just the words.
- Don't rebut.

Rules for both:

- The speaker has the floor.
- The speaker keeps the floor while the listener paraphrases.
- Share the floor.

The first time we taught this skill at a Marriage Alive seminar, we decided to demonstrate it for the group. Since we are often spontaneous and usually talk about whatever is presently going on in our marriage, it wasn't unexpected that I (Claudia) looked over at Dave and said, "What do you want to discuss using the floor?" This is the dialogue that followed:

• • •

Dave (speaker): Let's use the floor to talk about our seatbelt issue.

Claudia (listener): You want to talk about seatbelts? You're saying that's an issue with us?

Dave (speaker): Yeah, I feel like it's become a power struggle. We get in the car to go somewhere and you immediately tell me to buckle up. I feel like you're trying to control me.

Claudia (listener): You see this as a power struggle—between us? Like I'm trying to control you?

Dave (speaker): Yes, that's how I feel. Sort of like you're trying to be my mother.

Claudia (listener): Oh my, I'm acting like your mother and you don't like it?

Dave (speaker): You've got that right! Here you take the floor. (*Dave passes the floor to Claudia. Now Claudia is the speaker and Dave is the listener.*)

Claudia (speaker): Wow, I didn't realize seatbelts were such an emotional issue. I wouldn't have said it is a power struggle.

Dave (listener): This caught you by surprise. You didn't see it as a power struggle.

Claudia (speaker): That's right. I have no desire to control you and I certainly don't want to be your mother. I want to be your wife!

Dave (listener): That's good to hear!

Claudia (speaker): Dave, you're supposed to paraphrase what I said!

Dave (listener): Okay, you don't want to control me or be my mother.

Claudia (speaker): Right. But I do have safety concerns. I'm afraid that when I'm not in the car you won't buckle up and you'll be in a terrible accident.

Dave (listener): You're really motivated to tell me to buckle my seatbelt out of concerns for my safety.

Claudia (speaker): Yes; it's not a power struggle.

• • •

About that time a woman on the first row said, "Dave, I'm a trauma nurse in the emergency room at a local hospital. Just last week a man was brought in paralyzed from the waist down. Driving out of his driveway, he was sideswiped by another car. He wasn't wearing a seatbelt."

I (Dave) knew I was outflanked and it was time to move on. But everyone seemed to understand how to use the floor. We did too. Right in the middle of leading our own seminar, we had for the first time really understood our seatbelt issue and how each felt about it. You can see how the issue was actually about deeper feelings of control and safety. Discovering the feelings we were experiencing in this situation took our relationship to a new deeper level. We could both say, "Yes, we won't let this be a power struggle."

Since using the speaker/listener technique to talk about our seatbelt issue, have we resolved the issue? Not completely, but we're making progress. It's probably something we will have to deal with for years to come, but we lowered our frustration level. The purpose of the speaker/listener technique is to gain insight into your spouse's feelings that often is enough to find resolution. Other times, you may need to address the topic again and formally go through the following steps for resolving a conflict. Either way, you have an opportunity to show love by honoring your partner's feelings.

The next time an issue comes up that you need to talk about, try using this technique. Just remember to separate discussing and defining the problem from any attempts to solve the problem. Once you both agree on what the issue is and you both understand each other's feelings and perspective (and the facts), you are ready to move on to solving the problem.

Four Steps for Solving Problems Together

We suggest following these four steps—illustrated above with the seatbelt issue—to solve problems together:

1. **Define the problem**. Write down the issue you want to resolve. For example:

> *We want to resolve the seatbelt issue so that Dave doesn't feel controlled and safety is taken seriously. We defined the problem by using the speaker-listener technique.*

2. **Identify who has the need**. Note who has the need for a solution to the problem and also how the other person contributes to the problem. For example:

> *Claudia wants Dave to be safe but he consistently forgets to buckle up. Dave wants Claudia to stop nagging him and acting like his mother.*

3. **Brainstorm solutions.** Make a long list—don't stop with a few ideas. Brainstorm all kinds of solutions, even the crazy ones—humor helps to relieve tension. Here are some of the suggestions from our seminar participants:

- *Race each other to buckle up.*
- *Claudia gives Dave intimacy coupons when he buckles up. (Dave's favorite suggestion!)*
- *Both buckle up before starting the car.*
- *When Dave forgets to buckle up, Claudia becomes a human shield with her arm across Dave's chest.*
- *When Dave buckles up, Claudia gives him a kiss.*
- *Claudia will give Dave a few seconds of grace before gently suggesting that he buckle up.*
- *Dave, just buckle up! (Claudia likes this one!)*

4. **Identify a plan of action.** From your list of possible solutions, choose one you both would like to try. If it works, great. If not, go back to your list and try another one. For example:

Realizing this is a safety issue to Claudia and a control issue to Dave, we both agreed to work at it. Claudia agreed to resist nagging Dave and to remind him gently when he forgets to buckle up. Dave agreed to work at remembering to buckle up.

Once you get to steps three and four, you'll likely discover that most solutions involve compromise. This is when you have the opportunity to give each other one of three gifts to reach a resolution:

- *Defer with the gift of love.* You could say, "This is just more important to you than it is to me, so I'll choose to go along with what you want to do." Over time, both partners should be giving gifts of love.
- *Agree to disagree with the gift of individuality.* We don't have to agree on everything. In some areas it's okay to agree to disagree. This may include some perpetual issues we need to let go of so we can move on with our lives.
- *Compromise with the gift of mutual giving.* We each can give a little and meet in the middle on this issue.

There are times when Dave feels more strongly about an issue and Claudia agrees to go along with him. Other times when Claudia has felt strongly about a decision, Dave has given her a gift of love. It's not always easy to discern what to do. At times, we have done our best to make the right decisions, yet experienced disappointing results. Do we give up on resolving conflict and seeking to make wise decisions? No! And neither should you.

Note from a Dating Couple

Sometimes the little things become big irritations. After dealing for years with the toothpaste roller vs. squeezer issue, my husband actually solved it for us. He simply opened another tube and we now have our "his" and "hers" tubes of toothpaste. Smartest move ever!

Problems that took years to develop won't be resolved in one four-step exercise—or in one day or one week. But you can turn the corner and together begin to work on resolving them. Remember, not all problems have a permanent solution. This is especially true if the issue is something only your spouse has the ability to address. And it's important to note that there are some issues that should never be tolerated, such as verbal abuse, domestic violence, and chronic adultery. However, for most disagreements and issues, working through problems together can be a great opportunity not only to strengthen your marriage but also to experience the healing power of forgiveness.

So what do you do if you reach a stalemate and you just can't seem to work things out? A professional counselor may give you short-term help. If you're going down a one-way street in the wrong direction, you don't need a pedestrian shouting at you that you're going the wrong way. What you really need is a friendly policeman to come along, stop the traffic, and help you get turned around. That's what a counselor can do for your marriage. But in most instances, if you are willing to pull together, to attack the problem and not each other, to process anger and work together at finding a solution, you can find one.

A Few Cautions

Caution 1: Even if you're managing your conflicts well, there may still be issues to deal with. For example, it's a problem if just one of you is continually giving in to the other. It's also a problem if you consistently choose to coexist on everything, or if you use compromise as a means of "horse trading" and manipulation. Power plays and attempts to manipulate destroy the potential for love and closeness in a relationship.

Caution 2: Deal with what you can and accept what you can't control or change.

Caution 3: Choose your timing wisely. Avoid raising emotional issues late at night or when you're tired, hungry, or already out of sorts. Your marriage will be stronger for it.

Caution 4: When appropriate, look to the one with more expertise in an area to find the best solutions.

●——●

You may have noticed that we don't talk about conflict resolution in terms of winning and losing. When one "wins," both lose. It might work in the short term, but the long-term consequences are never worth it. Plus, it leads to resentment that can sabotage your relationship.

Avoiding Resentment

Nelson Mandela wisely said, "Resentment is like drinking poison and then hoping it will kill your enemies."[8] Resentment is an emotion over which you have total control. You have a choice: you can either drink poison from the bottle of resentment, or you can face what makes you want to drink from the bottle of resentment in the first place. If you want to almost guarantee relationship failure, go ahead and take a deep drink of poison and then approach your spouse about what you think he or she is doing that is causing your resentment.

On the other hand, if you first try to understand the situation from your spouse's perspective, your chance of finding a way forward is much higher. There will, however, be certain issues that you may need to return to the shelf for another day, and there will even be some you will need to accept because they are never going to change. At that point you have to ask yourself if you want to drink poison from the resentment bottle or take a swig from the acceptance bottle for the rest of your life. Remember, our goal is not to share one mind about everything; some differences add spice to our marriage, and every marriage experiences problems.

Everybody Has Storms — and the Storms Do Pass

When marriage is good, it can be very, very good. But when marriage is bad, it can be very, very bad. However, just because you experience a day or two of bad storms doesn't mean you should bail on the cruise. If you do, you will miss out on some great days ahead.

Sociologist Linda Waite discovered that among couples who described their marriage as really bad, five years later, nearly 80 percent said it was good or really good. Sometimes you just have to hang on and stay in the boat until the storms pass.[9]

As long as we are alive, we will face hard situations, make difficult choices, and have problems to manage and/or solve. The dullest marriages on earth are the ones in which both spouses have decided merely to tolerate one another—no conflict but no intimacy either. Let us challenge you to work hard at discussing and solving problems as a couple. You can process your anger, frustrations, and differences and use them as a means to strive for intimacy. Your marriage is worth it!

Now turn to the Dating Guide and begin planning for Date Three. You, too, can learn to use anger and conflict to build your relationship.

Becoming an ENCOURAGER

We will never forget the knock on our door late one winter night many years ago when we were living in Vienna, Austria. As we groggily answered the door, we were both surprised and elated to see our American friends from Warsaw.

This was several years before the dissolution of the powerful Soviet Union (which you may have only read about in history books—we are old enough to have actually experienced it!). The Soviets were threatening to take over the Polish government, forcing officials to declare martial law to control a nervous citizenry and minimize rioting and political dissension. The newscasts were brimming with stories of unrest and tension; Poland was on the brink of disaster. Seeing Jeff and Amanda and their three small children at our door brought celebration and relief. We were so happy to know they were safe!

After they told us their story, we were doubly glad to have them in our home. "As we were leaving Warsaw," Amanda told us, "we actually passed lines of Soviet tanks rumbling into the city. It was frightening!"

"We didn't know what the situation would be at the border into Austria," Jeff continued. "We had to wait hours, but here we are!"

Jeff made a phone call and the next thing we knew, a reporter from a national news service knocked on our door. Jeff and Amanda handed him what turned out to be one of the first videos to make it out of Poland—proof of the turmoil and upheaval martial law had caused.

Jeff and Amanda were obviously distressed. Imagine being uprooted from your home, work, and friends — not knowing when or if you might ever be able to return. Add three small children, sickness, and other pressures to the mix, and our friends were near emotional bankruptcy. They needed time to think and regroup. A couple weeks later we encouraged them to take a few days away without their children.

Things looked bleak as they drove away that cold, January morning. Amanda was tired, depressed, and feeling guilty about leaving their children. An hour later they stopped for lunch, and for the next thirty minutes Jeff told Amanda the things he appreciated and admired about her. He liked the way she was always there for him, her sense of humor, her sensitivity to the children's needs, her vital faith in God, her pioneering spirit. Small things, big things, insignificant things — he went on and on describing what he appreciated about her.

What a significant difference that thirty minutes made in Amanda's outlook on life; it certainly set the stage for a great getaway. From the beginning of their time away, Amanda knew she was loved, admired, and respected. During their week together, Amanda wrote: "It's amazing how things come into focus when we take the time to be alone and encourage one another. We've had so much fun, but now we're ready to come home, even though we still must face unsolved problems and an uncertain future." Fortunately, several months later they were able to return to their home, their work, and their friends in Poland.

Now imagine how different their week away might have been if Jeff had started things off by saying something like this to Amanda: "Honey, you've just got to get control of yourself. Can't you stop crying? You're not coping well at all. This just isn't like you. Your attitude is having a negative effect on our children and even on me! If you tried harder, I know you could control your emotions." The week would have been a first-class disaster, right? And Amanda would have felt even more insecure and depressed.

Here's the principle that Jeff and Amanda's story demonstrates: What we focus on grows. If you want a marriage garden full of weeds, focus on your partner's faults. If you want flowers, focus your thoughts and efforts on the flowers. Appreciation and encouragement is so powerful. Just like watering your flowers on a regular basis enables them to grow and thrive, expressing appreciation on a regular basis helps your relationship to grow and thrive.

So be proactive and look for ways to encourage and affirm each other. If you don't, who will? Your boss and coworkers? Don't count on it! Your children and teenagers? Ridiculous! What about your friends or even your friends on Facebook? Maybe or maybe not. Read on.

We recently read about an interesting experiment conducted by Facebook. For one week in January, 2012, Facebook data scientists manipulated the newsfeeds of 689,003 users, removing either all of the positive posts or all of the negative posts to see how it affected their moods. Researchers found that emotions were contagious. When positive posts were reduced, people produced fewer positive posts and more negative posts; when negative expressions were reduced, the opposite pattern occurred.[1]

We're not sure this research project was ethical, but it does demonstrate the power of positive input even with something as trivial as a social media newsfeed. Imagine the impact your loving and personal input could have on your relationship with your spouse!

Here are four strategies to help you give your partner the encouragement he or she needs: look for the positive, give honest praise, be a little creative, and learn to laugh together.

Look for the Positive

Before the wedding, it's easy to see only the positives in our beloved. We're on our best behavior and trying to hide or minimize our faults. When we were falling in love, we were literally in an altered mental state. We actually become intoxicated with love. The neurochemistry of the romantic love hormone cocktail bathes the brain for around two years. So when we looked at each other through rose-colored glasses, we were too drunk on love to see the faults that might otherwise have been readily apparent.

Once we marry and settle in to life together, this love hormone cocktail begins to fade. Did you, like us, discover the person you thought was just about perfect also had some irritating habits? The reality of living together creates tension, and it's easy to focus on the negative instead of the positive. Why does this happen? Look at the box below.

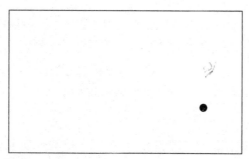

Where did your eyes immediately focus? The small, dark spot, right? We tend to ignore all the light areas and see only the dark spot. In the same way, we tend to concentrate on our mate's faults or weaknesses. Why? Could it be that our own insecurities are showing? It's hard to encourage when you feel insecure. If you are wrestling with personal problems, one of the most helpful things you can do for your marriage is to seek help from a counselor or a psychologist. However, for more routine issues, most of us simply need to refocus our attention on looking for the positive.

Johann Wolfgang von Goethe, the great German poet and philosopher, said, "If you treat a man as he is, he will stay as he is. If you treat him as if he were what he ought to be and could be, he will become that bigger and better man." The same principle applies to your spouse. Begin to look at your partner through Goethe's eyes. Maybe your spouse is taking a risk. Perhaps he or she is learning a new skill or even making a career change. Acknowledging and affirming your mate's strengths and his or her desire to grow and change is a great way to start focusing on the positive.

All of us bring some mix of strengths and weaknesses to our relationships. Ideally, we need to let each other operate out of areas of strength. (In the next chapter we will look closer at how to do this.) But even in our weak areas we can learn from each other. How? Consider how you might respond to two scenarios.

Scenario 1: Your mate is a stickler for organization, and you are the epitome of the maxim, "Creative people are not neat." Would you:

- Not even try to be organized because you don't want to compete with your spouse?
- Criticize your spouse for being too organized?
- Let your spouse know you appreciate his or her gift of organization and try to learn something from it?

Scenario 2: You love being a hermit, but your spouse is a gifted and gregarious conversationalist. Would you:

- Criticize your spouse for being too talkative?
- Send your spouse alone as your representative to all social functions?
- Appreciate your spouse's natural talent, express your appreciation, and challenge yourself to grow by learning from his or her insights and example?

Every day we make choices either to feel threatened by or to benefit from our partner's strengths. Do you encourage and appreciate the strengths your partner brings to your marriage partnership? If so, it will help you through the hard times. When you're willing to affirm each other's strengths, you may find that some of your roughest times become some of the best times in your marriage. Here are two practical tips that will help you develop the habit of affirming your spouse.

Track your positives and negatives. In his book *Why Marriages Succeed or Fail*, Dr. John Gottman says, "You must have at least five times as many positive as negative moments together if your marriage is to be stable."[2] Too often in marriage, the ratio of positive to negative is one to five; not five to one. What would your ratio be? Check it out. For the next twenty-four hours keep track of the number of positive and negative things you say to your spouse. Remember that five to one is just staying even. A higher ratio is much better!

Make a positive list. When we think negatively, it's easy to express our negative thoughts, but when we have positive, tender thoughts, we too often keep them to ourselves. To develop the positive habit, begin by making a list of ten to fifteen things you appreciate about your spouse. Then every day for the next three weeks, write down five things you appreciate about your spouse. They could be thoughtful actions or qualities you appreciate about your partner. At the end of each day, share at least one or two items from the list with your spouse.

Keep your daily lists and when you feel yourself becoming negative, pull them out and read them. It can change your perspective as you concentrate on your partner's positive qualities. Keep on turning those positive thoughts into words. Think of it as a positive recycle bin. Develop the habit of praising each other.

Give Honest Praise

The word praise comes from a Latin word for "worth," indicating a vital connection between the two. When we praise someone we value him or her. Descriptive verbs for praise are *commend* and *compliment*. Antonyms for praise are *blame* and *condemn*. It's easy to see which actions will build up and encourage!

Let us add our own definition of praise. Praise is describing what you appreciate. Honest praise is the opposite of flattery. Flattery is counterfeit praise. It makes the recipient feel uncomfortable and manipulated. Flattery is insincere and excessive praise, especially given to further one's own interest. Here are some practical tips for insuring that your praise is sincere.

SAY IT OUT LOUD

You can have all kinds of nice thoughts about your spouse, but he or she will never know it unless you say them aloud. Couples in a *10 Great Dates* small group were studying how to encourage their spouses. Most admitted that they had not developed the habit of praise. They each agreed to give their mates five compliments during the next week. At the end of the week, one wife confided, "It felt strange to hear the words come out of my mouth, but as I said them, it helped me see my husband in a more positive light."

Husbands especially need compliments. In general, men receive fewer compliments from people than their spouse receives. For instance, it's more common for a friend or coworker to compliment a woman on her appearance. It's awkward for men to compliment each other like that. So a woman might receive a few compliments outside of her home, but a husband is receiving compliments only from his wife. This is one reason it's important for wives to compliment their husbands—especially on their physical appearance!

Think about today or yesterday. Did you criticize your partner? Were you generous with positive words? Were those words general or specific? The most encouraging praise is also the most specific. For example:

"I appreciate your initiative and creativity in our sexual relationship."

"I appreciate your thoughtfulness in calling me when you're going to be late."

"I like the way you listen to me when I tell you what's on my heart."

Another tip when giving praise is to describe instead of compare. Comparison can lead to trouble. For example, you might say to your spouse, "You are the best kisser in the whole world!" In addition to being insincere flattery, this could cause your spouse to wonder, *How would you know?* or *And just who are you comparing me with?* It would be much better to say, "I like the way you kiss me." This is honest praise, and we all appreciate getting an honest compliment.

If we work hard to improve in an area, it's great to have a spouse notice. A few years ago, motivated by a back injury, Claudia worked faithfully on her physical fitness. She lifted weights, exercised regularly, and walked fifteen-minute miles. While her major motivation was to have a healthy back, the side benefits included better muscle tone, less flab, and a lower number on the bathroom scale. As I (Dave) began to notice these changes, Claudia appreciated my positive comments like: "Hey, you look great in those jeans."

WRITE IT DOWN

Keep the praise flowing by writing it down. Send short emails or instant messages of encouragement. Consider leaving little notes around the house for your spouse to discover. Sometimes we take our own advice. We still do this stuff.

I (Claudia) recently met a friend for lunch and left my car parked in a strip mall a couple miles from our home. Dave was aware of my plans, but I wasn't aware of his. Imagine my surprise when I returned to my car to find a note on the windshield. At first I panicked and thought I parked in the wrong place and had gotten a ticket. But much to my relief, surprise, and enjoyment, it was a note that read:

> *Would the cute, perky, young lady who owns this car please give me a call. I think we have a lot in common and should "connect" if you get my drift.* ☺
>
> *From definitely an adoring admirer.*

It worked. I hurried home! Take the time today to write a love note and to brainstorm other ways you can encourage your spouse. Here's what our creative friend Kelsey did to celebrate her husband's birthday.

Note from a Dating Couple

We use a notebook to write back and forth to each other. One of us will write something and then put it somewhere to surprise the other (under a pillow, in a cabinet or dresser, and sometimes in the fridge). It's always fun to find. Then, the other person writes something back and hides it again. It keeps the conversation going even when we are apart from each other most of the day. And it's a keepsake. This notebook is something we will cherish forever. We got this idea from my parents. Except they keep the notebook next to the toilet and write something to the other when "sitting" there for a while. Hah!

Be a Little Creative

We never know what our creative friend Kelsey will do next, but this idea of hers is a winner when it comes to affirming a spouse. She made the decision for her husband's birthday not to give just another material thing as a gift, but something unique from her and about their relationship. She filled a large plastic prescription bottle with small folded slips of paper. On the medicine bottle she wrote:

> For: ZACH
> RX: GOOD FOR THE HEART
> "Appreciation Medication"
> Read one Appreciation as needed
> Generic for Matrimonial Gratitude
> For Refills, call Kelsey

She took him to dinner at one of his favorite restaurants and presented her husband with his new "medication" and asked him to take (read) several before dinner. Later in the evening over dessert, she had him read a few more. Here is a sampling of her Appreciation Medication. Each represented something she appreciated about him:

- Giving me nightly back massages
- Getting stuff out of the top kitchen cabinets for me that I can't reach
- Maintaining the swimming pool
- Doing chores when I was sick
- Expressing appreciation for my cooking
- Popping popcorn for our Saturday Nights at the Movies
- Carrying out the recycle bin each week
- Babysitting our grandchildren with me

Yes, they have grandchildren, have been married many years, and are still encouraging each other. Maybe you want to come up with your own "Heart Appreciation Medication" for your spouse. Or make it a coupon book. Coupons are always fun to get. Your book might include coupons for:

- One back rub with hot oil
- Breakfast in bed
- Dinner for two at your favorite restaurant
- A five-mile hike together

Another idea is to give a gift for no reason at all. Once, on a promotional offer from a local department store, I (Dave) bought several small sample bottles of perfume and lotion. I wrapped each one individually, and each evening I hid one under Claudia's pillow. The first night, she was surprised; the second night, she was more surprised; and the third and fourth nights, she even went to bed earlier.

Just this past week at a discount store, I (Claudia) picked up a little travel bottle of Dave's favorite Burberry cologne. (Now we can both smell nice.) Since it was a tiny bottle, it wasn't expensive and it will pass the "three ounces or less" test going through airport security. He was surprised and appreciated me thinking of him. It was just a little thing, but love lives and thrives when we generously give little positives to each other on a regular basis.

One word of caution: If your spouse reads this chapter and you begin to get little gifts, cards, and extra attention, enjoy it. Please don't say, "I know you're only doing this because you read that book!" Instead, express your gratitude in your own creative way and be thankful for such a thoughtful partner.

Learn to Laugh Together

Laughter is a first cousin to encouragement. There are times in life when you can choose to either laugh or cry or just be frustrated. We try to choose laughter—like our recent nine-hour flight to Munich. We ended up sitting in "economy minus"—as in not "economy plus"—seats. For $200 we could have moved up two rows to "economy plus" seats, but $200 for an extra six inches for the next nine hours didn't sound like a good deal to us. We decided to make the best of it. Claudia pulled out her travel gear—her inflatable foot rest, lumbar and neck support, and "First Class Sleeper." (First Class? Who are they trying to kid?) When she inflated all her pillows, no space was left for Claudia. Time to regroup. That's when we declared this flight our "Cuddle Date." You don't need a lot of room to cuddle, and putting a dating spin on our tight quarters helped us to keep an okay attitude. Of course, we took selfies to document our date.

Laughing together and putting a positive spin on difficult situations dispels tension. It's good for your physical health, and it's definitely good for the health of your marriage. Give yourself permission to be less than perfect. No one is perfect. Not you or your spouse! When you don't take yourself so seriously, you can relax, and it is easier to laugh and see the lighter side of life. Humor is also a powerful outlet for tension. If joking comes naturally for you, consider yourself fortunate. But remember there is a fine line between jokes and insults. Laugh *with* your mate but only *at* yourself. It's definitely worth working to develop a sense of humor.

A couple weeks later on the way back from Europe, we had another "make the best of it date" — our all-day "Airport Date." Our flight was delayed five hours and you can only do so much in the Munich airport. I know it's cheesy, but we went to several gates and pretended we were saying good-bye to each other. You can hug and kiss and no one seems to notice or care. Next we had a fun "Window Shopping Date." We looked at all the expensive watches and picked out one for each other, which obviously we didn't buy. The airline provided us with meal vouchers so we had a Lunch Date. (The food was oh so much better than airplane food!) Finally, our flight was called, which turned out to be our "Getting in Shape Date." Because the plane was so late, it had no slot at the gate; we had to carry our heavy hand luggage down four flights of stairs, board a bus that was more like a "stuffed can of people," and then climb up the steps to board the plane.

We survived our airport date, but once home we both came down with a virus we think we picked up on the flight home. We drew the line at having a "Go to the Doctor Date," although we did go together.

Oh, the joys of traveling! We would happily resign from the jet set and pack away Claudia's inflatables, but then it would just be something else. We all have difficult situations in our lives. If we can step back, not take ourselves so seriously, and find something to laugh about, we can keep our relationship on a more positive track. Now it's your turn to come up with your own ideas and strategies for encouraging each other.

Dating is an attitude. You can turn a frustrating situation into a date.

Note from a Dating Couple

One thing we do is look for something funny throughout the day to tell each other over dinner. It helps us to find things to laugh about and we always love hearing each other's stories.

Now It's Your Turn

We have challenged you to look for the positive, to give honest praise, to be a little creative, and to learn to laugh together. The next time you find yourself in a really frustrating situation, try turning it into a date. Now it's your turn to put these ideas and strategies into action.

We close this chapter with a challenge: Write a letter of encouragement to your spouse. A favorite part of our Marriage Alive seminar is when the couples write a letter of affirmation to each other. Then, several months later, we drop their letters in the mail.

Tyler and Nicole told us how excited—and frustrated—they were when their letters arrived. Nicole said, "We were delighted to get our letters, but the day they arrived was one of those really crazy days. We were both in the middle of big projects at work, and that was the week our three girls had what seemed like an extra twenty-five activities at school. They needed a full-time chauffeur, and I was elected. Tyler and I decided not to open our letters but instead, to save them for a time when we could be alone. A few weeks later, Tyler's parents invited our daughters to spend a weekend with them. We saw this as a great opportunity for a getaway. I made reservations at a quaint bed and breakfast in the mountains. Fortunately, we remembered to bring our letters. The first night after a romantic dinner we opened and read our letters."

"From that point on the evening just got better," Tyler said with a smile.

You don't have to wait for a seminar. You can write a letter to your partner right now and describe what you appreciate about him or her. What personality traits attracted you to your spouse? If you mail it—especially if you send it to an office address—write "personal" on the envelope. (These letters have sometimes been intercepted by the wrong person and ended up on company bulletin boards!) Stamp your letter and mail it the old-fashioned way through the postal service. These days we tend to just get junk mail, so a personal note is a day brightener. Your partner just may write you back.

Note from a Dating Couple

As I was writing my letter to my wife, I suddenly realized that if anything happened to me, it's down on paper what she means to me and how much I love her.

Now it's up to you. Make your own positive list. Write your own letter. Look for humor and laugh together. Encourage your spouse today. Your marriage will be better for it.

It's time for Date Four. Turn to your Dating Guide and get ready to encourage and to be encouraged!

Finding Unity in Our
DIVERSITY

We can relate to the old adage, "Opposites attract." It perfectly describes us. When we first met, I (Dave) loved Claudia's creative and "can-do" attitude. I never had to worry about what to do on a date. She had ideas on top of ideas as well as the energy to plan and carry them out.

I (Claudia) loved Dave's easygoing and laid-back personality. He was never in a hurry and was such a good listener. He made me laugh and it was so much fun being with him. Totally relaxing.

Then we got married and soon discovered that the very things that attracted us to each other before marriage became irritations after marriage. I redefined Dave's easygoing ways as being too slow and blasé, and it frustrated me that all my activity and planning only served to tire him out.

For the first few years of our marriage, we tried to change each other. No big surprise it didn't work. I (Dave) didn't understand why Claudia couldn't just "laugh things off" and not take life so seriously. I (Claudia) wanted Dave to be more introspective and analytical—and to move a bit faster.

And then a job change required us to take a battery of psychological tests. We still remember the day we filled out those tests. I (Dave) nonchalantly checked off my answers while watching a football game on television while Claudia carefully considered each answer and crosschecked them for consistency.

Dr. Blandau, a psychologist, interviewed us the next week. He sat at his desk looking at our test results. "Dave, here are your strong points." As he listed them, I began to feel better and better. He went on, "Now here are the areas in which you are weak." That wasn't nearly as enjoyable to hear, but he was right on target!

Then he went through the same procedure with Claudia, listing her strengths and weaknesses. Looking at both of us he said, "Dave and Claudia, here are the areas you agree on, and here are the areas in which you tend to have problems." His accuracy was uncanny — he didn't miss anything. Our respect for psychological tests went up about 300 percent. Then he gave us one of the most beneficial challenges of our lives: "You probably noticed, Dave, that your weak areas are Claudia's strengths, and Claudia, that your weak areas are Dave's strengths. If you will allow each other to operate in your areas of strengths and not be threatened by the other, you have the potential for building a great marriage partnership."

We would like to say that we instantly applied his advice, but it didn't happen quite like that. It's hard to admit your weakness is your mate's strength. It took time and practice, and at times it was awkward, but we eventually did take Dr. Blandau's challenge seriously. We knew we would be a stronger team if we could follow his advice. Nevertheless, this is an ongoing process. We still work at applying his wise advice, but every time we do, it's beneficial. Allow us to share an example.

For years we published a monthly newsletter that was a perpetual source of frustration and conflict. Writing newsletters was not my (Dave) favorite activity, yet for some reason writing the newsletter landed in my to-do box. Claudia's gentle and not-so-gentle prodding did not help motivate me. However, once I finally sat down to write, I tended to overwrite, ending up with a newsletter much too long and crowded with details.

Then I would give the letter to Claudia. A natural-born editor, she would offer her expertise: "It's much too long. Why did you include this part? Delete this. Here, I'll help you." At that point, I just wanted only to be left alone. (The turtle withdrew.) I knew Claudia enjoyed writing, but I wasn't benefiting from her strength.

Finally, one day (when we weren't currently involved in writing a newsletter) we decided to reevaluate our strategy. Since Claudia really enjoyed writing, why not switch? Together we planned the agenda for each letter. Then Claudia wrote the first draft. I discovered I was a better editor than writer. Also I enjoyed managing the mailing list and taking care of details to publish it online and send it out as snail mail for the few who preferred the printed edition.

Changing our newsletter strategy to concentrate on each other's strengths had three positive results. First, our newsletters improved. Second, our relationship improved. And third, as we both used our strengths, we learned from each other. Over the years my writing has become clearer and more concise. Now we write books together. Claudia has become better with details and even enjoys formatting blogs for our website and e-newsletter. (You can check them out at 10GreatDates.org.)

Discovering Your Couple Strengths and Assets

Let us encourage you to assess your strengths and weaknesses and to operate in areas of strength as much as possible. You probably don't need a battery of psychological tests to determine your basic strengths and weaknesses. However, if you have the opportunity to take such tests, please do so. One online inventory that can help you identify your similarities and differences is the Couple Checkup at couplecheckup.com.

As you begin to identify your couple strengths, your differences can help you balance each other—especially if you appreciate those differences and don't feel threatened by them. In areas where you have similar strengths, you may need to look for ways to work together harmoniously.

One of the most helpful tools we've discovered for identifying couple strengths and assets is a series of eight continuums. Each continuum diagrams a polarity. For example, private/public, early bird/night owl, saver/spender. Though some continuums have gender tendencies, the many exceptions make generalizations untenable. Also, from time to time, we may find ourselves at different places on these continuums. For example, in some contexts you may be very extroverted or public, and at other times introverted or private.

As you consider each of the following seven continuums, think about your own marriage. Both sides of each continuum have strengths and weaknesses, advantages and disadvantages. Which side you or your partner tend to be on is less important than understanding that people are different.

Identifying where you are on each continuum will help you to be more intentional about balancing each other. Imagine that each continuum is a seesaw. If you are on opposite ends, you can enjoy the give and take of balancing one another's strengths and weaknesses. If you are both on the same side of the seesaw continuum, you will need to work on ways to share your mutual strengths and compensate for your shared weaknesses. The first continuum we will look at is private/public.

PRIVATE/PUBLIC

Are you private or public? Just think about how you use social media. Public people like to tell the world about how much they love their spouse, giving every little detail about a romantic getaway. Private people, on the other hand, would rather not have the world know anything about their special times together.

Introverted or private people are energized by times alone, while extroverted or public people are energized by being with people. It turns out there is actually a biological component to your tendency to be private or public. Did you know that it's possible to use MRI imaging to observe the differences in the prefrontal cortex part of the brain that codes the value of external rewards? It appears that extraverts are more motivated and energized by external rewards while introverts have a less active external reward system and find vigorous social interactions exhausting and need to be alone to charge their batteries.[1]

When couples don't realize their introversion or extroversion is innate, they can get very frustrated with their spouse for not having the same experience (biologically speaking) as they do.

Consider Brandon and Kirsten, who are at opposite ends of this continuum. Brandon loves people and is continually inviting others to join them for meals, vacations, outings—whatever. Kirsten is more private and just wants to spend time alone with Brandon. One of her favorite tricks is to kidnap Brandon for an overnight getaway. Brandon and Kirsten work to find balance without one person overpowering the other by respecting each other's preferences and trying to have both types of interactions. Often, compromise helps them find balance between the extremes of being either too involved or too uninvolved with others.

Another couple, Tyson and Katelyn, are both private. They like to be alone and tend to avoid socializing in groups. In fact, they'd like nothing better than to live on a desert island by themselves! Tyson and Katelyn naturally protect their private times, but they could benefit from more involvement with others. We suggested joining a couple's Bible study group, taking line dancing lessons, or making a list of couples they want to get to know and occasionally inviting one over for dinner or Bible study.

Kelly and Mike are just the opposite of Tyson and Katelyn—both fall on the public end of the continuum. As far as they're concerned, the more people they spend time with, the better. What's a vacation without friends? They are energized by others, care deeply for others, and are involved in other people's lives. To achieve balance, Kelly and Mike need to plan time alone. Relationships are built in twos, and they need to be sure to plan enough "two" time to keep their marriage healthy and growing.

Where do you and your spouse fall on this continuum?

PRIVATE	PUBLIC

If you are both private or both public, how might you compensate? Tyson and Katelyn now compensate by planning a couple of activities each month that include others. Last month, for example, they invited another couple to go antiquing together.

If you are opposites, how can you balance each other? For instance, each of you might plan one activity for the next few weeks. One might choose having friends over for dinner and the other might plan a date to go hiking on a remote trail.

SPONTANEOUS/PLANNER

For spontaneous people, life tends to just happen—they enjoy being unfettered by daily drudgery. Because spontaneity (sometimes described as impulsive behavior) is a way of life, the fun, exciting things tend to get done while the more mundane tasks of life—making a grocery list, paying the bills, doing the laundry—are typically ignored.

Planners like structure and may feel anxious or threatened by too much ambiguity. They are usually orderly and prefer to do things the same way time and time again. Interruptions are to be avoided and can create irritation and tension if they prevent a planner from carrying out the plan.

Where are you on this continuum?

SPONTANEOUS	PLANNER

If you are both spontaneous or both planners, how can you compensate? For instance, if you're both spontaneous, you could agree to check with each other before making any new commitments. Or if you're both planners, you could surprise your mate with a special night out. Whatever you plan will be "planned" for you but will be spontaneous for your mate!

If you're opposites, how might you balance each other? Perhaps the planner can defer to the spontaneous one, who says, "Why cook dinner tonight? Let's go out to eat." On the other hand, the spontaneous mate can agree to sit down and write out plans for the next week—"Next Friday we'll grill fish."

LIVE WIRE/LAID-BACK

Live wires are energetic and sometimes unpredictable. They are continually in motion and tend to be goal-oriented. If those around live wires are not focused, the live wires will happily organize them. Live wires have an overabundance of ideas and the energy to put many of them into action.

Laid-back people are calm and easy to be around. They are flexible and rarely rattled by life's demands. They tend to be great listeners, which is one reason many successful counselors have these attributes.

In our relationship, Claudia is the live wire. She doesn't even like to take naps during the day for fear she might miss something. Dave is the laid-back partner. He would much rather just let life happen. He marches to a slower (but consistent) drummer. He is methodical and persistent and likes to cross all the t's and dot all the i's. On this continuum we benefit from each other's perspective and balance each other most of the time—but not always! For example, when Claudia gets super-focused on a project, she loses all track of time and can work nonstop for hours without a break. Dave, however, will stop in the middle and take a fifteen-minute nap. It drives Claudia crazy. Or when we are trying to meet a deadline, Claudia will just hit the high points, while Dave gets upset because the details are missing!

Where do you fall on the following continuum?

LIVE WIRE	LAID-BACK

If you are both active and assertive or both laid-back and calm, how can you compensate? Do you need to slow down or speed up? Do you need to cut your twelve-hour day? If you're opposites, how might you balance each other? One way we balance each other is that Dave oversees details that demand consistency, like keeping up with our monthly obligations and managing our calendar, while Claudia helps us keep the big picture in view. She is the one to say, "Let's talk about our commitments for next year and how much traveling is reasonable." Dave, on the other hand, would say, "What about the details of today?" Dave also calms Claudia down when she gets hyper. At other times, Claudia motivates Dave to be a little more proactive rather than passive.

EARLY BIRD/NIGHT OWL

Psychologists tell us we are born with an innate time orientation. What is yours? Are you most engaged and productive in the morning, afternoon, or evening?

This continuum is perhaps the easiest to identify, but the hardest to balance. In our relationship, Claudia is the early bird and I (Dave) am the night owl. She prefers that I to go to bed early with her. I prefer her to stay up later with me. When we were first married, we tried to change each other—it didn't work. But through the years we have continued to work on synchronizing our clocks. We find ways to compromise when possible and accept each other when compromising doesn't work. To this day we haven't found the perfect solution, but we have managed to keep bedtime from becoming a battle or thorny issue.

Where do you fall on this continuum?

EARLY BIRD	NIGHT OWL

If you're both early birds or both night owls, how might you compensate? Many times a job or other life circumstance will do this for you. One of our night-owl friends is a surgeon who must be up early for surgery and hospital calls. His wife, also a night owl, tries to adjust her schedule. On vacations and off-the-job times, they can stay up all night and sleep all day!

If you are opposites, how might you balance each other? When we had teenagers at home, it was easy for Dave to stay up until they arrived home. When they got home, they knew their dad would be there waiting to welcome them, give them a hug, and check their breath for any hint of alcohol. Claudia had morning duty when one of the boys needed an early-morning send-off for a school or sports trip. It helped to acknowledge that we were different and that we weren't going to change the other—no matter how hard we tried.

Note from a Dating Couple

I so identify with Claudia and my husband is like Dave. I want to go to bed around 9:30 pm and my husband wants to stay up later. I feel like I'm always nagging him to come to bed because this is our time to talk about our day without any distractions. He wants to stay up until about 11:00 in order to de-stress from the day by doing things like playing a game on his tablet, reading a book, or working on a project. Eleven o'clock is too late for me since I have to get up in the middle of the night with the baby. This date helped us to talk about our situation and we hope to use what we've learned to manage our differences and see where we might be able to compromise or change our expectations.

FEELINGS-ORIENTED/FACTS-ORIENTED

Feelings-oriented people tend to express their emotions easily. They like an emotionally positive and open atmosphere and work quickly to clear the air if tension enters the relationship. They desire to work through conflict and "not let the sun go down on" their anger. Feelings-oriented people are focused more on relationships than facts.

Facts-oriented people speak in order to communicate information more than to express their feelings. They would prefer to avoid unpleasant feelings and become uncomfortable when emotional subjects arise. Their preference is maintaining a peaceful coexistence rather than confronting difficult emotions directly. Facts-oriented people are focused more on information than relationships.

Suppose you are trying to reach a solution to a problem. One of you is facts-oriented, the other is feelings-oriented. Your different perspectives can be beneficial. If a decision is made purely on feelings, you may be in for trouble. On the other hand, if a decision is based entirely on facts, you may be ignoring important qualitative input. Consider a couple trying to choose between preschools for their three-year-old son. If the facts-oriented spouse made the decision alone, the most influential factors would likely be cost, proximity to home, compatibility of scheduling, and parent-to-teacher ratio. If the feelings-oriented spouse made the decision alone, the most influential factors would be more subjective: cheerful rooms, caring teachers, and evidence of happy and contented children. All of these factors are relevant and necessary to making a thorough, balanced decision. One way of thinking is no more or less important than the other.

Where are you on this continuum?

FEELINGS-ORIENTED	FACTS-ORIENTED

Do you balance each other or are you both on the same side? For example, if you are both feelings-oriented, it's easy to get caught up in the excitement of the moment and overlook facts, like a couple we know who were shopping for a new car. They both got carried away and committed themselves to buying a new car on a used-car budget. They ignored their financial reality and ended up with large car payments that drained their limited resources. The next time they shop for a car, they will compensate for their weakness by doing their financial homework and deciding just how much they can spend before they hit the car lots.

On the other hand, if you are both facts-oriented, making decisions based solely on facts is often unwise. There are often significant emotional or relational factors that need to be considered. Like in the car-buying example, if only facts had been considered, the couple may have purchased a car they could afford but that they both hated to drive. So the next time you are faced with an important decision, discuss both the factual and emotional aspects of the issue. The quantitative factors will be easy, but you may need to dig deeper to unearth the qualitative or emotional factors.

TIME-FOCUSED/NOT TIME-FOCUSED

Here is another continuum on which we differ. While we have found some benefits, we've also had to manage irritations. I (Claudia) live by the clock. My motto is: "Early is on time and on time is late." Dave is the classic "non-timed" person. Time—what's that? Fortunately, he sets alarms and reminders on his smart phone that help keep him on track.

Where are you on this continuum?

TIME-FOCUSED	NOT TIME-FOCUSED

If you are both time-focused or both not time-focused, how might you compensate? If you are opposites, how might you balance each other? For those really important occasions—like appointments—Dave works at being punctual. For other occasions that are not so important, Claudia tries to be more flexible.

SAVER/SPENDER

Saving money energizes some. Spending it energizes others. Katie and Benjamin struggle with being on opposite ends of the spender/saver continuum. Katie comes from a family where money grew on trees. If there were blank checks in the checkbook, there must be money in the checking account, right? Benjamin's penny-pinching family took "frugal" to a whole new level. They dried paper towels to reuse! The couple's challenge is to balance Katie's spendthrift tendency with Benjamin's miser tendency.

Where would you place yourself on this continuum?

SAVER	SPENDER

If you and your spouse are opposites, it may be easier for you to find balance than if you are both savers or both spenders. The key is to work together to find balance.

As you process and seek to balance the ways you and your partner are different, keep in mind that your goal is not to be the same. You were created with differences, and your differences bring balance to your marriage. Looking at the ways you are alike and the ways you are different is simply a means to help you identify and focus on your couple strengths.

As we noted in chapter 4, what you focus on grows. If you view your partner's differences as weaknesses and focus on them, problems are sure to follow. Such focusing on weaknesses is like poking an open sore. It doesn't bring healing. Over several decades of leading our marriage seminars, we have observed that couples are helped much more by concentrating on their combined strengths, seeing these as their couple assets, than by pointing out the other's weaknesses. When partners concentrate on each other's strengths, an amazing thing happens: they learn from each other.

Let us share one more observation. A strength taken to an extreme can also be a weakness. For example, a perfectionist who is consumed by getting every detail right may never get anything accomplished. As a couple, you have the wonderful opportunity to balance each other and combine your assets, but you should also be prepared to handle some inappropriate reactions both from yourself and from your partner. (We'll talk more about this in chapter 9.)

Psychologist Revisited

Many years after we took that battery of psychological tests, we had the opportunity to retake them and to sit down for yet another consultation with Dr. Blandau. We were surprised and pleased to learn that we had actually learned a great deal from one another. Our weak areas were not as weak. We were a stronger team. We had proven it works!

Do you see ways your differences complement each other and may give balance to your marriage team? Together you can discover ways to compensate for areas in which you may be too much alike. Appreciate the uniqueness of your team and be intentional about looking for hidden assets. If you are willing to learn and grow together, we can guarantee you will be amazed at the couple treasures you discover! In fact, we believe that your greatest assets are your differences. Now get ready to talk about them!

Turn to Date Five in the Dating Guide. A great date on appreciating your differences awaits you.

Building a Creative
LOVE LIFE

One of the most difficult parts of marriage is keeping romance and desire alive over the years. When a *Ladies Home Journal* poll asked 1,500 readers in their thirties and forties, "What is your idea of a perfect evening?" would you believe only 7 percent responded, "Romance and making love"? Eighty-nine percent said they were stressed out some or most of the time, so no wonder sex was at the bottom of the list![1]

Stress, lack of time (and lack of effort), exhaustion, anxiety, health issues, and even "that time of the month" can lead to the loss of emotional connectedness and wreak havoc on sexual desire. Plus, it's normal for the intensity of sexual desire to drop when the "love cocktail" we mentioned earlier begins to wear off after a couple of years. Also a low level of desire for women is an issue for over 40 percent of women and 20 percent of men.

While this may not be the most encouraging news, it can be reassuring to realize, "Hey, I'm normal. Others feel as I do." The question then becomes, what can be done to restore the passion and desire if it's not where you would like it to be?

The best thing you can do for your marriage is to *stop having sex* and instead *start making love*. If having sex is more about you and your pleasure, then you will never get to experience the ecstasy of connecting with your spouse on a deeper physical and emotional level. That only comes when you're making love to your spouse and the focus of your thoughts are on your spouse and not on yourself. When you reach this level of lovemaking, you will agree that it is far more satisfying than any sexual experience you have had.

Having logged several decades together, we can tell you from experience that reaching this level of intimacy is hard, but not impossible—especially if you have the determination to stay romantically connected through the years. If you ignore your love life at any stage, your relationship can become stale, boring, and anything but romantic. Before you know it, you're thinking, *What happened? Where did the romance, fun, and intimacy go?*

The Marital Drift

We married while in college and knew zilch about how to build a creative love life. We soon discovered that romance, intimacy, and great sex didn't come automatically with our marriage license. About the time we were finally getting it all together, the children starting arriving. Like many parents, we found the early parenting years challenging as our care-giving roles took center stage.

At this stage of marriage, many couples stop touching. Their sex life gets put on the back burner. Life happens. Romance and intimacy fade. The enemy—boredom—creeps in. It's at this point couples need to guard against "adventure lust." Affairs usually don't happen overnight, but spouses who are tired, isolated, and romantically starved are vulnerable.

Pornography is another dangerous desire killer—and now it's available 24/7 from the comfort of your own home. Pornography is highly addictive and can spell the death of intimacy and desire in a marriage.

The research is now clear that porn rewires the sexual response cycle in the brain for both men and women. The deeper the addiction gets, the more women report a lack of desire for their spouse, a decrease in lubrication, and so on. And for men, not only is there a decrease in desire, but a greater likelihood of porn-induced erectile dysfunction (ED)—and Viagra can do nothing to help because porn-induced ED is a psychological, not physiological, problem. The rate of porn-induced ED is rapidly increasing among both younger and older males. Once the brain has been rewired by the graphic intensity of modern porn, it's difficult for the real thing to elicit a sexual response.[2]

So how can you avoid the dangerous potholes of boredom, adventure lust, affairs, and pornography? How can you build a more creative love life and reclaim intimacy and romance? A great place to start is by understanding six key components that nurture love and romance.

Six Components of a Romantic love life

Keeping your love life alive and thriving is about far more than sex. One of the greatest rewards of building a creative love life is truly knowing and being known by your partner and becoming one flesh. An intimate and creative love life is multi-dimensional and encompasses far more than the physical act. Consider the following components necessary for having a thriving and creative love life.[3]

TRUST: FEELING SAFE WITH EACH OTHER

Trust is essential for the health of your marriage. You need to know you are safe with that other person. When trust is broken, it's important to address and repair it quickly. Keeping short accounts will go a long way to rebuilding and then maintaining trust. Remember, "love covers over a multitude of sins."[4] Work at building and reinforcing the trust that exists between you. Here are a few simple trust builders:

- Being quick to apologize when you're wrong;
- Offering a helping hand when your partner is stressed out;
- Giving an honest compliment;
- Keeping your sense of humor—especially when things go wrong;
- Letting your spouse know you have his or her back.

When you trust each other as you do life together, it's easier to be open to being more adventuresome and creative, which can result in a more romantic and rewarding love life.

MUTUALITY: FREELY CHOOSING TO LOVE EACH OTHER

Both people must want to be in this relationship. In marriage, we choose each other above all others. We commit to a mutual willingness to grow together and to adapt to each other's changing needs over the years. When you know you are mutually committed to one another, you don't have to use up precious time continually evaluating the relationship, asking, "Does he really love me?" or "Is she going to hang in there?" This requires being "other-centered." In a sexual relationship, it's easy to become "me-centered" and forget that the best way to really please ourselves is to please our mate. When we focus on mutually pleasing each other, we are less self-conscious. Think about how wonderful it is when your partner makes you feel loved and desired. A gentle caress, a smile across the room, or a loving comment makes you glad you're mutually devoted to each other. When you act on mutuality, you choose couplehood over individuality. You look for ways that you can please each other rather than yourself.

Here are a few ways to demonstrate your devotion:

- Going to the opera that she loves and you tolerate;
- Ordering his favorite pizza when you'd rather order Chinese;
- Framing a favorite picture of the two of you doing something together that you both enjoy;
- Writing a love note in the steam on the bathroom mirror;
- Showering your spouse with verbal affirmation;
- Sending a simple text message: "I'm thinking of you and can't wait to get home tonight."

When you are mutually devoted to each other and really enjoy being together, you will feel more confident and secure in your love life. This can foster creativity and can definitely be a romance enhancer.

HONESTY: OPENLY COMMUNICATING YOUR TRUE FEELINGS

Truthfully sharing your feelings, needs, and desires with each other (without manipulation) will help your love life grow and bloom. It is possible to speak the truth in love. You can start by following the guidelines in "Smart Tips for Great Dates" (page 160).

Early in our marriage we agreed to talk openly about our love life. In some ways, talking about sex was like learning a new language. We had to develop our vocabulary, and then we had to use it! How would we know what the other liked unless we talked about it? We also talked about our fears and inhibitions. Claudia was more inhibited than I (Dave) was, so a major part of "talking it out" was me being willing to listen to Claudia. Here are some tips that might help you to communicate your honest feelings:

- Develop your own secret phrases or code words that are only meaningful to you. ("Feeding the birds" was one of ours, but it's secret so we can't tell you what it means.)
- Start your sentences with "I."
- Avoid starting your sentences with "you" and "why."
- Read a book or blog on sex aloud together.
- Share with each other what you really like about your love life.

It takes commitment, intentionality, and openness to be honest with each other, but the rewards for your love life will be significant. You won't spend a lot of time doubting and misunderstanding one another. Plus, it leaves more time for love! It was wise King Solomon who said, "An honest answer is like a kiss on the lips."[5]

INTIMACY: KNOWING AND BEING KNOWN

Intimacy is that intangible quality of unity, understanding, and synergy that moves two people from being acquaintances or friends to being lovers and soul mates. Intimacy may be a higher need for one than the other, but it's vitally important for both.

Note from a Dating Couple

In our relationship, I tend to be more visual, and when I think about romance I think about physical intimacy. On the other hand, my wife responds more to tenderness and talk. When she thinks about romance, she's thinking about emotional intimacy.

When intimacy is low in a relationship, partners aren't as motivated to talk to each other or touch each other in loving and caring ways. Couples who experience a high level of intimacy often are more affectionate, laugh louder, and are more likely to feel understood, accepted, and loved. So be intentional and work at being an intimate couple. Here are some ways to invest in your own couple synergy:

- Write an old-fashioned love note (on paper with a pen).
- Take a walk and share your dreams with each other.
- Listen with your heart. (This means seeking to understand what your partner means by what he is saying and trying to understand his perspective.)
- Gaze into each other's eyes for five minutes without saying anything. Just let your eyes do the talking.

Like the other components of a creative love life, intimacy can ebb and flow over the years. Maintaining a healthy level of intimacy requires time and effort, but the rewards are great as you share together your dreams, needs, fears, and longings with one another.

SENSUALITY: GIVING AND RECEIVING PLEASURE

Sensuality involves touching, holding hands, hugging, and caressing in a pleasurable way. Touching is a significant means of connection and bonding.

Note from a Dating Couple

After having this date, we discovered you really can add more sensuality to your relationship. Recently, as we were enjoying dinner at our favorite restaurant, we began to play "footsy" under the table. Later, we drove home and lingered in the car for a few minutes sharing hugs and kisses and well—we were amazed at how something so simple kindled our desire!

Here are some ways to add a little sensuality to your relationship—maybe tonight!

- Cuddle on the couch.
- Listen to your favorite relaxing and romantic music together.
- Light scented candles.
- Wash your partner's hair.
- Share a decadent chocolate dessert.
- Practice the twenty-second hug and ten-second kiss.

If sensuality is a challenge, set aside private time. Explore each other's bodies to discover what feels good and what doesn't. Sound simple? Maybe not! One thing that can help is to plan times of "non-demand touching," which is touching that does not have intercourse as its objective. (It actually stirs up oxytocin and dopamine.) You may discover that the more cuddling and passionate kissing you engage in that *doesn't* result in intercourse, the more you may actually desire physical intimacy.

If you've lost that sensual feeling, you can recapture it. We often recommend that couples try practicing the Sensate-Focus Exercise.[6] The purpose of this exercise is twofold: to keep you focused on sensuality and touching in your physical relationship and to help you talk more openly and naturally about likes and dislikes in your lovemaking.

As with non-demand touching, the Sensate-Focus Exercise isn't about sexual intercourse. That would defeat the purpose because the focus is on sensuality. The goal is to relax and experience this exercise in a way that you each enjoy.

The idea is that you take turns giving and receiving pleasure. One is the giver and one is the receiver until you switch roles halfway through the exercise. When you are the receiver, your job is to enjoy the touching and tell your spouse what feels good and what doesn't. You can give either verbal or nonverbal feedback by gently moving your partner's hand around the part of the body being massaged to provide feedback about what feels good. As the giver, your focus is to give pleasure by touching your partner and being responsive to feedback. It's fine to ask for feedback and focus on what your partner is wanting.

Before you start, choose roles and give a massage of hands or feet for about ten to twenty minutes, asking for and giving feedback. For the first few times, try massaging areas like the hands, back, legs and feet to get comfortable with this technique. Remember to switch roles halfway through.

You may want to try the Sensate-Focus exercise several times a week over the course of several weeks. If you are relaxing and all is going well, you can begin to move to other areas of touching. Wherever you want to be touched is great. Over time, you can work on both giving and receiving at the same time, keeping the emphasis on sensuality and communicating your desires. If you practice this exercise consistently, it will become easier to talk openly about touch. It will also add vitality to your lovemaking and increase your desire to love and be loved.[7]

SEX: JOINING TOGETHER PHYSICALLY

The culmination of a great love life is sexual intercourse. It is the most intense and intimate experience a couple can share. In their book *The Good Marriage*, Judith Wallerstein and Sandra Blakeslee emphasize the importance of sex. "In a good marriage, sex and love are inseparable. Sex serves a very serious function in maintaining both the quality and stability of the relationship, replenishing emotional reserves, and strengthening the marital bond."[8]

Having a creative love life is not an optional add-on to marriage or a selfish physical desire; it's a vital part of growing and solidifying your marriage for a lifetime. But what about couples where one or both of the partners face physical limitations? What happens when our libido changes through the years? How do we handle the fact that the sexual desires of the typical husband and wife are seldom at the same level? These challenges can be overcome. Don't join the ranks of the many couples who give up and settle for a tepid or nonexistent love life.

Remember, making love is about far more than having sex. The couples with the best sex lives are the ones who have figured out that there are many ways to make love besides intercourse. So whatever challenges life throws your way, don't give up on loving each other. Take some time and be proactive today. Here are some ideas to upgrade your love life:

- Give yourself the gift of uninterrupted time together. Send the kids to the grandparents for the evening (or if you have no family close by, adopt some grandparents who love your kids).
- Give a sensuous massage to get into the mood.
- Schedule sex. Add times for loving to your calendars. (This may not sound romantic, but it works!)
- Just do it. You'll be surprised how much you may enjoy the results!

Take the challenge and prioritize physical intimacy. Keep it safe. Nurture it. Be intentional about cultivating trust, mutuality, honesty, intimacy, sensuality, and sex as essential vitamins that will strengthen your marriage. Take them regularly—and watch your love life bloom and grow. If you're up for the challenge, there are some practical things you can do to keep your love life healthy and growing.

Two Habits to Keep Your Love Life Hot

Often in our seminars we tell couples, "It's not a matter of *knowing* what to do as much as it's a matter of *doing* what we know." In the last few pages we've explored the different aspects of building a creative love life, including numerous practical suggestions for "doing what you know." Now it's time do what you know by developing the habit of making your love life a priority and romancing your spouse. Let the fun begin.

PRIORITIZE YOUR LOVE LIFE

Too often lesser things take precedence over the sexual relationship. You want to work on it but don't set aside time alone together. Remember, it takes time to communicate, to work through conflict, and to build a creative love life. Let us encourage you to make your love life a high priority. Your sex life can be a growing, exciting part of your marriage. It can happen even with little children. Here's how we did it.

We carved out a regular time each week when we could be alone without the children. One year we instigated "Monday Mornings." All three children were in kindergarten or at Mom's Day Out. The house was ours. We discovered that there is nothing sacred about making love at night. Monday mornings were great! Your schedule may not be as flexible as ours, but find what works for you. For example, maybe you can hire a babysitter to take your kids to the park (or somewhere else if the weather is inclement) for a couple of hours on Saturday mornings.

We also started a tradition of going off alone together once or twice a year. Sometimes it was just overnight; other times it was the whole weekend; occasionally we got away for a whole week. We realized that we needed extended times alone together—more than just a morning. So we looked for opportunities to get away. We couldn't afford to hire a sitter to come and stay with our children for an extended time, and our parents lived too far away. But we did have friends—very good friends—who offered to keep our three sons. We reciprocated by keeping their two girls, and we're sure we got the better deal!

Years later, two of our early getaways stand out in our memories, but for very different reasons. On the first getaway alone and without our children, we went to a lake cabin in Alabama for the whole weekend. It was "love city" from the time we got there to the time we left! Dave remembers the Alabama weekend as very fulfilling. Claudia remembers being oh-so exhausted.

We spent the second memorable getaway at the beach in Florida. Claudia fondly remembers the slow pace of life, the long walks on the beach, romantic interludes, candlelit dinners for two, shopping together, and buying a new dress. Dave remembers it as a great week, too, but years later confided he was a little disappointed that we didn't make love every day we were there.

If we could live those years over again, we would talk more about our expectations and what is realistic for us. (We probably would have ended up in Georgia—halfway between Alabama and Florida!) The key is to prioritize your love life by finding a plan that works for you.

Talk about your unique situation and what you can do to make your marriage and your romantic life a high-priority love affair. Share your expectations so that unmet or unrealistic expectations don't lead to resentment—resentment will extinguish any flame of passion and desire in your marriage. You can nip resentment in the bud by being willing to talk openly and freely about your expectations.

Now, where in your weekly schedule can you carve out some just-for-two loving time?

Note from a Dating Couple

For us, sex releases so much tension and stress in such a unifying way that most of the things that bothered us before no longer even matter. It helps us remember how dependent we are on each other, and how supportive and beautiful love can be to help us get through those difficult times.

ROMANCE YOUR SPOUSE

Once prioritizing times together is a habit, here are four ways you can romance your spouse.

Step out of your comfort zone. Don't settle for the same-old romance routine—add some intrigue by doing the unexpected. In her book *Dating in Captivity*, psychotherapist Esther Perel writes about "erotic intelligence" and encourages couples to cultivate playfulness, curiosity, and even a bit of drama which can lead to anticipation and being more erotic and romantic with each other.[9]

I (Claudia) will never forget the day years ago when Dave approached me with three red roses and said, "Pack your bag. We're leaving in thirty minutes!" Remember, Dave is the romantic. Off we went to a wonderful little hotel in the mountains about an hour from where we lived. I wondered why they looked at me so curiously when we checked in. Dave had previously chosen the hotel and told them he had a very special lady friend he wanted to bring for a getaway. To this day, I'm convinced that the hotel staff didn't think we were married. Dave's reaction? "If you're going to have a romantic affair, have it with your spouse!" And that's just what we did.

Try new things. Move your lovemaking to new settings. Try out rooms in your house other than your bedroom and see what appeals to you. For instance:

- Consider that swing you just added to your secluded screened porch.
- Why not initiate that new rug?
- What about an evening of non-demand touching under bubbles in a candlelit bubble bath?
- Try a game in which the loser must strip — one game you can both win.

Not all of these suggestions originate with us. We heard some of them at a follow-up group of one of our Marriage Alive seminars. The seminar had taken place eight months previously, and this particular group had gotten together each month to share and encourage one another to continue having great dates.

This particular evening each couple brought something that represented their marriage. One couple brought a green potted plant to suggest a growing marriage. Another couple brought a devotional book and shared how they were now praying together.

Amazingly, over half of the group shared something about adding creativity to their love life. From hotel receipts to whipped cream — this group was creative! But Brant and Amber took the prize. They brought a tuxedo apron, a chef's hat, and a bottle of lotion. This empty-nest couple told the following story.

One evening after work, Brant volunteered to prepare dinner. Amber, exhausted from her day at work, stretched out on their newly carpeted living-room floor and fell asleep. Imagine her surprise when Brant woke her up wearing only the tuxedo apron and chef's hat, with lotion in hand all ready to give her a body massage! Creativity was alive and well!

Upgrade your bedroom. Make some changes to create a more

romantic atmosphere, like adding scented candles, music, a dimmer switch, and a lock on the door. Remove all the books and paper work. And most important, forget about your to-do list when you are behind closed doors. You might even want to make your own "do not disturb" sign. We saw one recently in a hotel room that said, "You don't even want to think about coming in here right now."

Work at overcoming obstacles. When we asked a friend how she keeps romance alive, she immediately replied, "Live in two countries." She and her husband temporarily have jobs in two different countries and are forever having to overcome obstacles simply to be together. Most of us won't have to overcome something so drastic, but all couples — especially parents of young children — need to work to overcome the obstacles life throws at them. The harder you work to be together, the more precious the time together will be.

A creative, enjoyable, and satisfying love life is not a marital add-on. Far from it. It's one of the keys to a healthy alive marriage. So give yourself permission to prioritize your love life and romance your spouse. And remember to have fun in the process!

Loving for a Lifetime

Loving for a lifetime may just make your "lifetime" longer and a lot more enjoyable. According to a ten-year study in Germany, men who kissed their wives before leaving for work lived, on average, five years longer and earned 20 to 30 percent more than peers who left without kissing good-bye. The researchers also reported that not kissing before leaving in the morning increased the possibility of a car accident by 50 percent. This makes sense to us. Couples who kiss before leaving for work in the morning are more likely to begin the day with a positive attitude, leading to a healthier lifestyle.

Also, couples in their forties, fifties, and sixties who keep their sex life alive report far more satisfying and better sex than anything they ever had in their twenties. And if you want to look ten years younger, just keep on loving each other. It's far better, safer, and less expensive than Botox — with none of the side effects.

And here's some surprising good news for couples in long-term marriages. Recent research reveals that on average couples who make it to fifty years of marriage start to see an increase in the amount of sex they have.[10] That's yet another good reason to keep investing in regular physical intimacy over the years of your marriage.

Now it's your choice. What will you decide? Your sex life can be as fulfilling and exciting as you want to make it. It takes time and work but it's worth it. It can become better, more intimate, and more wonderful as the years go by.

Note from a Dating Couple

We have found through our five years of marriage that without intentional time spent together loving each other, we have more reasons to nitpick each other's faults rather than overlook them and see our positive traits. When we make time for each other, even if it is just to snuggle on the couch for our favorite T.V. show, then we have more reason to sleep soundly and another reason to wake up grateful.

Now is your opportunity to plan a great date! Maybe you will want to even kidnap your spouse for a weekend away. For additional ideas, turn to Date Six in the Dating Guide.

DATE SEVEN

Sharing Responsibility and WORKING TOGETHER

The focus of Date Six was building a more creative love life, but wait,—there's more encouragement on this topic. Did you know that research reveals that couples who more equally share the workload at home have better sex? That makes sense to us. When partners share the workload, both have more time and energy. So maybe there is something really sexy when your partner pushes the vacuum or does the dishes!

I (Dave) am the "kitchen elf." A number of years ago we made a deal—Claudia cooks and I clean up. This scheme works pretty well for us, I sometimes need to be reminded. Like the time we moved down the street to a new house. We got out of our routine and after a couple of days Claudia commented, "I don't think the kitchen elf got the directions to our new home. Have you heard anything from him?"

I responded, "No, but I bet if you baked some chocolate chip cookies, he might smell them and find his way here." I didn't really think she would take my suggestion seriously, but later that day when I came in the door my nose led me straight to the kitchen where I was greeted with a platter of warm cookies, complete with a cold glass of milk! Coincidently, that very same evening, the kitchen elf returned.

Seriously, we both benefit when we tackle responsibilities and work together as a team. It would be easier to do if we had more hours in our days, but guess what, we don't! Plus, so many couples both work full-time outside the home. Others who don't work outside the home might be running a home-based business or home schooling their children or caring for a special-needs child or elderly parent. Life gets complicated. At times like these, couples need to pull together so nobody falls apart.

We remember one Marriage Alive seminar that was filled with frustrated two-career couples complaining about the stresses of trying to hold it together at work and at home. There was simply not enough margin to make their lives work.

If you are among the many couples who struggle with balancing your responsibilities and sharing the workload at home, we hope this date will help you to find balance and to devise a plan that works for you.

Balancing Your Responsibilities

In order to balance your responsibilities with your spouse, begin by assessing your current division of labor. You may want to consider your responsibilities outside of the home as well as your responsibilities inside the home. If you were to collect all your various responsibilities (including jobs) on either side of a seesaw—yours on one end and your spouse's on the other—would your seesaw balance?

For instance, if one spouse is working part-time and the other is working a sixty-hour week, the one working part-time would likely need to help balance the seesaw by carrying more of the load at home. But for now, let's assume you both have equal commitments outside the home. The important question then becomes, How are you pulling together as a team?

Before their children came along, both Scott and Lindsey held jobs outside the home. When they started their family, they decided Lindsey would put a hold on her teaching career so she could stay home with their three kids and be a full-time parent. But halfway through the parenting years their circumstances changed. When Scott's company downsized, he kept his job, but his bonuses were eliminated. Lindsey went back to teaching to help meet expenses and to save for their children's college expenses.

Scott's daily routine didn't change. He worked as hard as ever at his job and came home just as tired, but Lindsey's daily schedule changed drastically. Five days a week she came home tired, had lesson plans to prepare for the next day, and still faced the same responsibilities at home—not the least of which was what they were going to have each night for dinner. Scott was understanding and didn't say much about the frozen dinners, but not having clean socks and underwear irritated him. Tension built, and by the time Scott and Lindsey came to our marriage seminar, they needed help. We encouraged them to make a list of their current responsibilities— and ask themselves if they needed to make some adjustments.

ASSESSING YOUR RESPONSIBILITIES

A light went on when Scott and Lindsey evaluated their respective responsibilities. Their lists looked something like this:

Lindsey's Responsibilities at Home	Scott's Responsibilities at Home
1. Prepare meals	1. Take care of the yard
2. Run errands, buy groceries	2. Keep cars maintained
3. Do laundry for family of five	3. Keep family financial records
4. Clean house	4. Prepare annual tax return
5. Keep track of children's activities	5. Manage 401k and other long-term investments
6. Arrange for sitters	
7. Help children with homework	
8. Help kids with the bedtime routine	
9. Monitor kids' Internet, screen time, social media use, etc.	
10. Transport kids to activities	
11. Pay the bills	

In order to keep their home running smoothly, Scott and Lindsey needed to make some adjustments. Scott's home responsibilities were important and took time, but he could accomplish them on the weekends. Lindsey's areas of responsibility were not as flexible and demanded more time each day than she could give.

If you find yourself in a similar dilemma, set aside time to list all household tasks and responsibilities and the requirements for each. Then look at the list and talk about who naturally enjoys the various tasks—and which tasks you enjoy least. Then go through the list again, considering each task from the perspective of who can do the job better.

When we did this exercise, we discovered that Claudia doesn't mind doing the laundry, so she took that on. I (Dave) take care of the vacuuming. I'm also fine with keeping track of our finances—a job that's easy for me and gives Claudia headaches! While talking through our list, Claudia immediately conceded that I was the best bathroom cleaner in ten states! That was one job neither of us wanted to take on, but I usually do it and get extra brownie points.

Note from a Dating Couple

One of my friends recently complained about how mad she was at her husband for washing her son's clothes with the red towels. Now everything was pink! I'm sure she wanted my sympathy, but all I could think was "Wow, your husband does the laundry? Good for him!" My husband doesn't do the laundry, but after listing out our individual responsibilities, I have a greater appreciation for what he does do. And yes, after this date, we made some minor adjustments.

The brutal reality is that there will always be jobs nobody wants to do. Compromise is an important part of the process. You are also looking for understanding. We all handle stress better if just one other person understands how we feel. You can be that other person for your spouse.

Once Scott and Lindsey evaluated their situation, Scott understood the stress Lindsey was experiencing and the need for his increased participation at home. The solution to his "no clean socks and underwear" dilemma might have to be that he takes responsibility to wash them himself. But the mechanics of who does what are not as important as the deciding to attack the problem together.

Scott and Lindsey recruited their school-age children to help with jobs around the house. Lindsey was tired of teaching when she arrived home, but she loved being creative in the kitchen. So she bought cookbooks for easy, one-dish meals. Often with her slow cooker and a little planning, she had dinner underway before she left for work each day. Scott began to monitor the kids' homework and help with special school assignments. They hired a cleaning service once a month and found a teenager who loved yard work to do the routine mowing and mulching. Scott and Lindsey's seesaw responsibilities may still go up and down, but on any given day it's much more balanced.

AVOID SCORE KEEPING

Do what you can to balance your seesaw, but realize that things won't always balance out and it's best not to keep score. Sometimes it may seem like one of you is carrying a heavier load that the other, but there are often many things that go unnoticed and untallied. Obsession over keeping score and keeping the seesaw balanced can lead to anger and resentment. Why? Because your spouse will likely never do enough. It's all about perspective. The way you keep score is different than how your partner keeps score, so throw the scorecard away. Chances are your spouse is giving a lot more than you think he or she is. Another area where couples need to work together is managing money.

Note from a Dating Couple

For the first ten years of our marriage, I was nursing, changing diapers, and constantly holding a baby. I was totally flustered at church one day when a friend came up to me and said, "Your husband is so helpful with the kids. I really admire him for that!" I felt awful. I was so caught up in my own overwhelming frustrations and so focused on how hard I have it that I completely missed how good my husband is with the kids. To me, being a fun dad and playing with the kids is just as important and rewarding as helping me with the dishes.

But if I was so caught up in keeping score, I would be too upset to be grateful for that wonderful skill he has. This date helped us get on the same page and to appreciate each other's help a bit more.

——————•——————

Managing Our Money Together

One of the most common points of contention in many marriages is money. If money is a touchy subject in your marriage, we hope you can begin to talk about it on this date. Depending on your situation, you might also want to set up subsequent dates to talk more in-depth about your finances or to meet with a financial planner. You can also find many resources on budgeting and money management online, but for this date, here are some thoughts to help you just start the conversation. We suggest starting by defining your financial goals.

DEFINE YOUR FINANCIAL GOALS

Couples can reduce the amount of stress and tension related to finances by having well-defined, mutually agreed-upon financial goals. Setting goals together can be challenging, especially if one is a saver and the other a spender, but the benefits can be significant, not only to your relationship but also your financial future.

Start by making a list of potential short-term and long-term goals. A goal can be as simple as setting aside resources for a weekly date night or deciding what you're *not* going to spend money on. Setting financial goals together will help to reduce stress in your marriage. Did you realize that reducing your stress level can save you big bucks? When stressed, many people tend to soothe themselves by overspending.

Defining your financial goals together will also help you develop an "us against the problem" attitude. When you attack your financial challenges together, you can focus your energies on solutions instead of defending yourself or attacking your spouse. You may be amazed at the progress that can be made toward paying down debt or saving for a goal when you work together to manage your money. After we became parents, one of our first big financial goals was buying a house. Claudia was a substitute high school teacher, and we saved all of her paychecks for a down payment. We never fought over how to use that money because we'd already agreed how we were going to spend it. (Fortunately, back in those days, we were able to get a 100% VA loan.)

Once you define your financial goals, the next step is developing a plan to reach them.

GETTING STARTED MANAGING YOUR MONEY

With your financial goals identified, the next step is to develop a plan to implement them. You can find a number of helpful websites online for developing a budget and formulating your financial plan.[1]

We are not financial advisors. We don't have it all together in this area of our lives, but we continue to work on it. Here are a few recommendations we've found helpful. Start by tracking how you spend your money.

- *Periodically keep a record of each penny you spend.* One or two months of this will not only increase your awareness of what you spend but also help you evaluate where your money is really going. Then you can modify your spending and saving patterns, which is not so easy, but possible. Mint.com is a free resource that can help you track your spending.
- *Limit credit-card spending to what you can pay off each month.* If things are really tight, we try not to use credit cards. Somehow it's just easier to spend too much when buying with a credit card. And now you don't even need to pull out your card — all you have to do is swipe your smart phone. Maybe you justify by saying, "Well, I'll probably bring it back, and it'll be easier to return if I charge it." It may indeed be easier to buy, but a month later the bills arrive.
- *Consider using cash for your everyday expenses for a few weeks.* It will cause you to think twice about what you are purchasing as you watch it disappear from your wallet. It will also help you not to spend more than you make.

- *Develop the habit of saving, even if it's just a small amount.* If you live with less, you will have the ability to save a little each month. We used to say we couldn't afford to save. The truth is we can't afford *not* to save. How much we save is not as critical as developing the habit of saving. Consider long-term goals — such as retirement and your children's education. Also consider short-term goals. If you have older children, you may want to choose a family goal. For instance, you might have a family garage sale to help finance an upcoming family vacation.
- *Don't overlook the joy of giving.* Several couples we know also have a special bank account. Each month they put money in that account, and from it they support their church and favorite charities. Researchers have found money can buy happiness in only one scenario: when you are spending it on someone else.

We hope our brief thoughts on managing your money together will encourage you to define your financial goals and better manage your finances, but let us add one caution. In setting financial goals and working to achieve them, it is possible to acquire all the material things you would like to have but end up with added financial stress and too much stuff to maintain, which can be a drain on your marriage. Many financial problems in marriage could be lessened if we just learned to delay gratification and live with less.

DELAY GRATIFICATION

If you want to achieve your financial goals in your marriage, you need to learn to delay gratification. Daniel Goleman argues it's an essential part of emotional intelligence. He defines emotional intelligence as the ability "to motivate oneself and persist in the face of frustrations; to control impulse and delay gratification; to regulate one's moods; to empathize and to hope."[2]

Goleman correlates the ability to delay gratification with successful living, which includes the ability to develop strong marriages and families. But delaying gratification isn't easy when you live in an instant world with instant credit. If you are bored and have the right card, you can whisk your spouse off to a romantic island — no need to get babysitters (if you have children) or even pack. We are told to "Just do it!" But real life doesn't work this way. Not in life and especially not in marriage!

Closely related to delaying gratification is learning to live with less. Living without something you've never had is not a huge sacrifice. We think of friends who are happily married and do a wonderful job of managing their money and living within their means. They live in a small home with one bath and no dishwasher and manage fine. They don't live with the stress of huge loans and repayment schedules.

We suggest it is never too late to learn to delay gratification. The ability to delay gratification is like a muscle. The more you use it the stronger it gets. So pick something this week and practice using your ability to delay gratification. This can be a real marriage builder, especially as you manage your money together. One last challenge is to choose your lifestyle carefully as the following couple did.

CHOOSE YOUR LIFESTYLE CAREFULLY

Before their children were born, Collin and Jennifer both had full-time jobs and experienced little financial stress, but now it seemed like they were continually struggling to make house payments and meet other financial obligations. Jennifer wanted to stay home with their two young boys, but it seemed impossible financially. After reexamining their priorities and financial goals, they realized that while home ownership was great, their higher priority was having more time to love and nurture their children. So they did a very brave thing: they sold their house and moved into a more affordable condo so Jennifer could stay home with their children. It was a tough choice, but at least they had choices.

When it comes to lifestyle, some of us have more choices, but we all have some choices. Lindsey went back to teaching to help provide for their family; Jennifer chose to stay home to nurture their preschoolers. Whatever your situation, you can find ways to work together. If you both work outside the home, do it from a united front. You'll need all the communication and negotiating skills you can muster. Evaluating your expectations and redefining your goals will be an ongoing process, just as it was for Justin and Melanie.

Both Justin and Melanie had jobs that required extensive travel, but neither was aware of how separate their lives had become. Then one day they met accidentally in the Los Angeles airport. Neither even knew the other was supposed to be in California! Melanie told us, "We looked at each other and realized we hardly knew each other anymore. We had homes, cars, boats, but we didn't have a vitalized marriage. Standing on that concourse, we agreed something had to change!"

"That was a turning point," Justin continued. "We evaluated our lifestyle and our list of necessities became much shorter. We are both cutting back and slowing down. We have a long way to go, but we are making progress—and we are getting reacquainted with each other!"

Do you need to get reacquainted with your spouse? We often hear, "We're working hard for our kids—to give them more advantages in life." Noted child psychologist Dr. T. Barry Brazelton said that one key to successful parenting is to spend half as much money on your kids and twice as much time. Maybe that's also a key to a vibrant marriage.

Only you can decide this highly personal issue, but it's important to make your decisions together. What things are most important to you? How important is owning your own home, driving a new car, having the latest smart phone, tablet or laptop, or owning the latest video game console, or largest smart TV? What about vacations and meals out or ordering meals in? Make your own list and then prioritize what's most important so you can let go of the rest. It's up to you—and you really do have the power to *choose* your life, no matter how limited your means may be. So look at your life, look at your marriage, and then chart your course.

NOW IT'S YOUR TURN TO CHOOSE

As you chart your course, be willing to compromise and choose a team approach. In your home responsibilities, choose to make adjustments where needed. You can share responsibility and work together both at home and in the financial realm. Choose marriage-friendly financial goals and be willing to delay gratification where needed. Working together may not be your easiest job, but it may be one of the most rewarding, for both your relationship and your financial future.

Now it's time for another great date! Turn to Date Seven in the Dating Guide and get ready to have fun working together and sharing responsibilities.

Balancing Your Roles as
PARTNER AND PARENT

If you don't have children—by choice or otherwise—you may be wondering if you should bypass this date. It can be a meaningful date if you look at it from a different perspective. If you aren't a parent, at least you have been the child. You can use this time to talk about how you relate to your own parents. (We understand that this topic can be a very sensitive area for some couples who are not parents. If you feel it would be best to skip over this date, we give you permission to do so.)

Consider where you are now in the family life cycle. Are you in the stressful baby and toddler years, the teenager years, or somewhere in between? Psychologists tell us the two times of greatest stress on a marriage are when you have toddlers and again when you have teens. If you have both at the same time, you have twice the challenge! Or maybe your kids are grown and you're in the empty nest or perhaps not-so-empty nest with boomerang kids or kids who never left. Or you may even be parenting a grandchild or caring for an aging parent.

Before we had children we dreamed about how great it would be to have kids. But when that first baby arrived, life changed—and not in the oh-so-dreamy ways we thought it would. This was a whole new balancing act, and our lives were never the same again! It's not easy to build your marriage while you parent your kids, but it is vital to both the health of your marriage and the health of your family that you try.

Mom can love the child and Dad can love the child, but unless Mom and Dad love each other, the child can feel insecure. Did you realize that the number-one fear of children is that their parents will get divorced? So never feel guilty working on your marriage. When you are working on your marriage, you're also working on your family! The two relationships can actually enrich each other.

A Painful Challenge

If you have been unable to conceive, you might talk about the challenges you face. If this is too painful, it's okay if you want to skip this date or substitute another topic.

We won't be sharing many parenting tips in this chapter, but we do want to share a new way of looking at your dual roles as partners and parents. First, we will consider how children can positively influence marriage, and then we'll talk about how the marriage partnership can positively influence children.

How Children Enrich Marriage

What has the energy of an atomic bomb, provides more entertainment than a Broadway show, and weighs about seven and a half pounds? It's that first baby! The first child brings big changes for Mom and Dad. Nothing is ever the same again.

Although we hear much about the strain parenting places on the marriage relationship, not much is said about how having children can enrich a marriage. Just observing our grandkids and their parents reminds us of ways parenting our own children enabled our marriage to grow. You can experience the same. Here are seven family-based marriage enrichers that we and other couples have experienced. As you reflect on each one, consider the ways your children enrich your marriage.

CHILDREN REMIND US THAT WE'RE ONE

Little ones running around are a continual reminder that you are "one." Each time you see Billy's toes, you have to admit they are just like Dad's, or that Susie's big smile is a picture of Mom's smile, which won you over years ago and still melts your heart.

Think about your children for a moment. What traits did each child get from your spouse? From you? Even if you have a blended family or if your children are adopted, you still pass on many of your traits and values to your children. Look for them. Compliment your mate when you have the opportunity. "Lacey laughs just like you do—it's contagious and makes me laugh, too"; or "Jessie's got your big blue eyes"; or "Jamie has your pleasant, easygoing personality. What a wonderful asset in getting along with people!" Affirm your great observations. It's fun to realize how your child is a blend of the two of you and that you truly are "one."

Note from a Dating Mom

I loved my husband as a newlywed, but when I saw him hold our son for the first time—this precious baby we created together—an indescribable wave of love for my husband came over me that I had never experienced before. Yes, having children has its challenges, but the joys you experience together because of them strengthens that love. Five children later, I will never forget that moment.

My mother-in-law says the same thing about my father-in-law now that she sees him as a grandpa playing with the grandkids. She says it is a complete turn-on for her! (Maybe "too much information," but even grandchildren strengthen relationships!)

CHILDREN FOSTER TEAMWORK

Parenting definitely calls for a team approach. It's difficult for one parent to do it all. As young parents, our evenings always went better when we helped each other. We both looked for solutions, and often came up with good ones. For example, we hired our eleven-year-old neighbor to come over and play with the kids during the "last nerve hour"—that hour in the late afternoon when Claudia was exhausted and just trying to get dinner on the table. Even giving your mate a coupon for one hour of "off-duty" solitude can strengthen your marriage team.

Think of how you can team up with your partner. Brainstorm ways to lessen stressful situations such as "morning madness." One of you might assume responsibility for breakfast while the other makes sure the kids get up, get dressed, and stay on schedule. At night when the kids are in bed, together you could talk about how to handle extra stresses you may be experiencing. Just knowing one other person understands your stress helps tremendously in handling it appropriately. When you have kids, there is less room for selfishness. It's not about what you want to do or what I want to do. It's about what is best for the child.

At this point we need to pause and address the elephant that may be in the room, which is your individual parenting style. Few parents look at parenting through the same lens, and differences can cause major conflict for many couples. And when couples don't discuss or manage those conflicts healthily, they tend to push each parent more to the extremes. So if one feels the other parent is too harsh, they may compensate by becoming more nurturing, and if one feels his or her partner is too soft, they may become more strict. Children can tell when they are the source of a conflict between their parents and it's hurtful to them.

If you need to talk about this issue, set another time rather than this date to talk about your parenting style and how to present a united front to your children. Use the communication skills you learned in Dates Two and Three to discuss your parenting styles and to manage parenting conflicts in a way that strengthens the relationship rather than damages it.

CHILDREN PROMOTE APPRECIATION

Because the responsibilities of parenting leave less free time for two, you'll learn to appreciate each other in a new way. Having time alone together is a worthwhile treat. When you have a few minutes, make a list of positive attributes that parenting brings out in your partner. For instance, "Hank's amazing patience with our children encourages me not to overreact when I get irritated with one of them." When you finally find those few minutes alone, share your thoughts.

Note from a Dating Mom

We have an eleven-month-old baby and I loved this date! I now have a new appreciation for both my baby and my husband.

CHILDREN PROMOTE CREATIVITY

Having small children will stretch your creativity. You'll think of all kinds of ways to spend time alone. In one Marriage Alive seminar filled with young parents, we asked for suggestions for finding time together. Megan, the mother of six-month-old twins, reminded the group that even some semi-alone time can be helpful. She suggested a stroller date. Your baby will enjoy the fresh air, and you'll enjoy the exercise and conversation. Other suggestions from the group included:

- Plan a "Progressive-Errand Date." Group your errands together. You can have time alone in the car as you visit the cleaners, post office, and drugstore. And on your way home, you can stop by the frozen yogurt stand.
- Grab that time when your kids are at soccer practice. If you need to be close by, walk around the field together and talk.
- Go to a park that has a tennis court. Give your children plenty of balls and the two of you can sit down and talk. The tennis court becomes a gigantic playpen!
- Plan a getaway the same weekend as the junior-high band trip.

Take advantage of the challenges children bring and keep looking for creative ways to find time for each other in the midst of the busy parenting years.

CHILDREN CHECK OUR COMMUNICATION AND KEEP US HONEST

It's amazing what you say or don't say when little ears are listening. You're the model. It's enough to make us all stop and think before we speak. Just doing that would benefit any marriage.

We learned how important it was to be on the same track and say the same thing. Kids will ask each of you the same question and then act on the answer they like best. Our boys made mincemeat out of us if we weren't united in our decisions and communication.

Children are a reality check. If our talk doesn't match our walk, little eyes will see and report it. You may tell your children it's wrong to lie, but they immediately note any contradictions. For example, have you ever told a child, "Tell him I'm not home," when the phone rings and it's someone you don't want to talk to? Or have you looked the other way when your ten-year-old wants to go to a PG–13 movie. Children need parents who are honest, consistent, and who admit it when they blow it.

You can use conversations with your children as a springboard to your own private conversations. Are your children helping you to say what you mean and mean what you say?

CHILDREN PREVENT BOREDOM

With children around, there is always something going on. You don't have to worry about sitting around in the evening and lamenting, "Oh, my, what can we do?" Also, children can help you relax and loosen up. Every family seems to have one joker who helps to keep things light and unpredictable. Your marriage will be more fun and less boring if you learn to laugh with your kids and at yourself.

CHILDREN GIVE GREAT REWARDS

Attending our youngest son's college graduation was a rewarding experience. As he and his classmates walked across the stage, there was a great sigh of collective relief from six hundred sets of parents.

It is rewarding to see children launched into adult life. And part of that reward is all the memories of how your children enriched your life and marriage. You'll never run out of things to reminisce about. But we also send them off into life with numerous ways our marriage has enriched their lives!

Tips for Harried Parents

When we had three children five and under, we had to discover how to find time to connect with each other in little places. One couple we know occasionally set their alarm for the middle of the night in order to spend uninterrupted time together. Here are some simple ways to focus on your partner when the days are long and you are weary:

- *Snuggle before going to sleep.*
- *Lie on a blanket in front of the fireplace; put the blanket outside when it's warm so you can gaze up at the stars.*
- *Turn off screens and look into each other's eyes without talking.*
- *Share two cups of chai or hot chocolate, light a candle, and listen to music.*

When we had adolescents, there were other stresses to deal with— mostly to do with angst and drama. It's easy to get caught up in it all. But don't let your teen's problems overwhelm you. Remember, this is a temporary stage. They do grow up and leave home. Here are a few ways to find some partner time in the midst of these stressful years:

- *Use times when your kids are at school activities. You don't have to be at every practice game or choir rehearsal.*
- *Look for alone time in the cracks, like when your teen sleeps in late on Saturday morning.*
- *"Soundproof" your bedroom. A stereo system or radio provides a noise buffer and adds to your privacy.*
- *Look for humor. Finding humor in the middle of a stressful situation can help dispel it. Laughter actually helps us relax. During these years, don't take yourself or your kids too seriously. Much of what you are experiencing is temporary—this too shall pass.*

How Marriage Enriches Children

One of the greatest gifts we can give our children is a happy home with parents who love and respect each other. We've said it before, but it's worth repeating: The best way to help our children build successful marriages is to have one. An enriched marriage lived out before them day by day by day will fortify their marriage with all kinds of vitamins. We love one of the illustrations we use in our Marriage Alive seminar. A couple is kissing in the kitchen and the caption reads, "Be good parents. Gross out your kids!" It certainly adds to their sense of security that Mom and Dad really do love each other and are here to stay. Here are five ways marriage can enrich your child's adult life and marriage.

WE PROVIDE SECURITY, LOVE, AND A SENSE OF BELONGING

From Abraham Maslow's research on the hierarchy of human needs, the family provides those basic needs—home, shelter, safety, food, and clothing.[1] But it doesn't stop there. A healthy, enriched marriage provides children with a unique sense of security and love. As our children sense our love for each other, they are enveloped in that love. With this foundation, they develop a sense of belonging and identity. Marriage gives us a unique opportunity to influence the next generation and pass down a legacy of love.

WE MODEL HEALTHY RELATIONSHIPS

We do know that attitudes are caught, not taught. It's not so much what you say as what you model. Do you openly give and receive affection? One of Dave's best childhood memories is seeing his parents out on the balcony, kissing and hugging each other. In a culture characterized by high rates of divorce, kids feel secure when they are assured by actions—not just words—that Mom and Dad love each other.

Your children learn how to build healthy relationships by watching you and your spouse relate to each other in your marriage. Being able to relate to others positively is one of the great gifts we can give our children.

What are you modeling to your children? Is most of the communication they hear relayed in the connecting style, the chattering style, or the confronting style? From you they learn how to express their own feelings and deal with anger in a positive way. When our children were young, we taught them the feelings formula (from Date Two) and often reminded them to practice it by saying something like, "I hear some strong feelings and that's okay, but could you state that again and begin your sentence with 'I'?" Not only did it help our communication with our children, it also helped our children in their friendships and dating life as they grew and matured.

Note from a Dating Couple

Our kids know that Friday night is Mom and Dad's date night. Whether we get a babysitter or not, they know it's our special time together. It's important that the kids know we make our marriage a priority.

WE GIVE GUIDANCE AND LEADERSHIP

As parents we are there to give guidance to our children. It is extremely confusing, however, if Mom and Dad are giving different responses to questions or conflicting advice for problems. When we are united, we send positive messages and our children learn that they can trust and rely on us. They know we aren't perfect, but they also know we are real and that we are united. This keeps open the lines of communication and, even as adults, they feel free to ask our opinions. (And occasionally we feel free to give them!)

WE TEACH LIFE SKILLS

The home is the first school for learning life skills. And since so many of those skills involve relationships, marriage is the ideal context from which to pass on life's most important lessons. You might want to make a list of lessons you learned from your parents. Then make a list of lessons you hope your children are learning from you. Things such as teamwork, stewardship, responsibility, boundaries, and ecology—the list could go on and on.

WE PASS ON TRADITIONS AND VALUES

What an opportunity we have in our marriages to pass on traditions and values to our children and their spouses and families! While our children are not clones and will not reflect all of our traditions and values, their core beliefs often come from the home they grew up in. As a couple, set aside some time to list your basic values and beliefs. What traditions are most precious to you? How do you model your core beliefs? Is it time to dig deeper and explore together the ultimate meaning of life? In the next chapter you will have the opportunity to do just that. In the meantime, enjoy counting the ways your marriage enriches your children and the ways your children enrich your marriage. Both you and your children benefit!

Looking Ahead to When the Kids Grow Up

Balancing your roles as partners and parents helps prepare you for when your children eventually grow up and leave the nest. Trust us, there's a wonderful second half of marriage out there just waiting for you! And how you learn to balance your roles now will make a big difference when you graduate from the active parenting years into the more supportive and encouraging years.

Research shows that the couples who invest in their marital relationship while their children are young are the empty-nest couples who have the most rewarding and satisfying marriages. It's like the principle of compounding interest. Making small investments when you are young enables you to enjoy the rewards that come later.

It is much more difficult to accumulate wealth the longer you wait to invest in your retirement account. And if you wait until retirement age to start investing, the chances of success are very small. The same principle applies to marriage. The couples who wait until they are empty nesters to invest in their relationship usually struggle to make the transition.

Time to Balance Your Act

Now it's the time to focus on your unique balancing act. Wherever you are in the family cycle—no kids, toddlers, or teens, a true empty nest, or nest refilled with adult children and/or grandchildren—there's always something to balance. The different stages of family life offer challenges and opportunities not only to positively influence your marriage but also for your marriage to positively influence the children around you. Be thankful for the opportunities ahead to balance your roles as partners and parents.

Influencing Other Children

If you haven't experienced parenthood (by choice or by being unable to conceive), consider how you can influence other children in your life like nieces, nephews, little neighbors and so on.

Turn to Date Eight in the Dating Guide and celebrate together how your children enrich your lives!

Connecting Faith, Love, and
MARRIAGE

Did you know that couples who pray together are likely to have deeper levels of emotional intimacy and even more frequent and satisfying physical intimacy? Also, those who are active in their faith are less likely to divorce, have higher levels of satisfaction, and higher levels of commitment.[1] In a survey of over 50,000 married couples, happy couples were more than twice as likely as unhappy couples (85 percent versus 40 percent) to report satisfaction with how they expressed their spiritual values and beliefs.[2] So it makes sense to talk about connecting faith, love, and marriage—and that's what you'll do on this date.

We realize that not everyone who experiences *10 Great Dates* will be religious or spiritually inclined. However, we believe all of us have a core belief system that shapes who we are, how we relate to others, the values we choose, and the choices we make.

Discovering Your Core Beliefs

What are your core beliefs? What do you believe about life, death, family, marriage, God and so on? Exploring these topics together can help you grow closer to each other. Drs. Les and Leslie Parrott shed light on the value of a shared commitment to spiritual discovery in their book *Saving Your Marriage Before It Starts*: "The spiritual dimension of marriage is a practical source of food for marital growth and health. No single factor does more to cultivate oneness and a meaningful sense of purpose in marriage than a shared commitment to spiritual discovery. It is the ultimate hunger of our souls."[3]

Wherever you are on your spiritual journey, talking about your core beliefs is a great starting place for connecting with one another spiritually. What fundamental values do you and your spouse share? What life principles do you both strive to apply in your marriage and family? On what aspects of your spiritual lives do you agree? If someone looked at your life, would they be able to discern your core beliefs? This is a challenging question—especially for those of us who profess faith in God.

Sean confided in us, "My wife and I both grew up going to church and made personal commitments to God while we were in high school. We're still involved in our church, but our faith is not something we really talk about with each other. I really would like to have a deeper spiritual connection with my wife but don't have a clue how to begin to do that."

Perhaps you can identify with Sean. If so, we have good news for you! There are four core values you can use to forge a deeper and more intimate spiritual connection: unconditional love and acceptance, forgiveness, prayer, and service. Talking about them together on this date can help you connect your faith, love, and marriage.

Unconditional Love and Acceptance

Have you tried to love your spouse unconditionally lately? We know it's not always easy. Too often it's, "I'll love you *if* ..." rather than "I'll love you *in spite of.* ..." Think back to Date Five. Are there differences in your personalities and approach to life that are hard to love and accept? As we said before, those things that attract us to each other before marriage often become irritations after marriage.

One thing we love about being in a long-term marriage is that it's easier to accept each other as a package deal. What were once viewed as the other's irritating traits we have reframed as "your loveable little idiosyncrasies." Do you need to do some reframing?

Two thousand years ago the apostle Paul gave some good advice to the people of Corinth who were having trouble loving each other unconditionally. He reminded them that love is patient and kind. When you really love someone, you don't envy him or her or get angry easily. Your love is to be forgiving, and you are not to keep track of wrongs or even notice the other's shortcomings.[4]

Does our love for each other line up with Paul's description? Not always! It's hard to love like that. It's certainly not natural, and in our experience it's the spiritual dimension of life that empowers us to live out this kind of love with each other. We have to realize continually that love is not just a feeling, but a choice we can make.

Note from a Dating Mom

Maybe it's because I am a mom, but it is through having children that I have learned what unconditional love truly is. Moms can relate to this tender feeling of loving our children. It is up to us to build on this gift of love God gives us as parents so we can also love our spouse unconditionally.

Forgiveness

Closely related to unconditional love and acceptance is the core value of forgiveness. Without forgiveness we can't build an intimate relationship with our partner or with God. No one is perfect, and we often let each other down. Show us a marriage without forgiveness and we'll show you a marriage with bitterness, disappointment, unresolved conflict, and little spiritual intimacy. When a long-term marriage crumbles, it's usually not the result of a major crisis or a one-time event. More likely it's the result of smaller issues left unaddressed that have built up and become big issues over time.

Drs. Markman, Stanley, and Blumberg remind us, "Forgiveness

is a core theme for relational health. Long-term healthy relationships need an element of forgiveness. Otherwise, emotional debts can be allowed to build up in ways that destroy the potential for intimacy.... Marriages need forgiveness to stay healthy over the long term."[5]

We have found that being willing to forgive each other and ask for forgiveness builds our relationship. As God forgives us, we can forgive each other. A forgiving spirit helps us to be more compassionate, tolerant, generous, and benevolent with each other. A friend of ours shared with us the following analogy of forgiveness.

Forgiveness is like dropping hot rocks. It just makes sense that if someone hands you a hot rock that is causing pain you would drop it as fast as possible. Yet when we are handed an emotional hot rock we tend to cling to it and even think crazy things like, *I am not going to drop this hot rock until you apologize.* Forgiveness is not for the person who offended you. It's really for you! Most of the time the other person doesn't even know you are clinging to the hot rocks, and even if you make it crystal clear, it doesn't help you in the process of dropping the hot rocks.

It could even be that you have been clinging to some of these rocks for decades. When we are in emotional pain from a hot rock, it is much harder to feel and express love. Even if you are able to drop the hot rock, you will still need to heal the scar with the healing balm of love. For rocks that seem impossible to release, the best thing to do is to turn to the source of forgiveness — the God who loves you unconditionally — and ask God to help you drop the rock and forgive. The answer to your prayer may not come immediately, but as you continue to ask for God's help, your heart will be transformed and the forgiveness you once thought impossible will then be possible. Even so, painful memories may linger. While God forgives and forgets, we mortals will still remember. But over time and as the memory fades, it becomes easier to realize that we have forgiven and the pain is diminished or may even go away entirely. In a loving relationship, most of the time the hot rocks our spouse hands us are unintentional, and just as we hope they would cut us some slack, we should cut them some slack as well.

Note from a Dating Couple

These twelve words help us to live out our forgiveness in our marriage:
"I am sorry, I was wrong, please forgive me, I love you."

DROPPING HOT ROCKS

Do you have a hot rock in your hand that you need to drop but you're not sure how to let it go? Start by acknowledging to yourself that you want to let go of the hurt that has become an obstacle in your marriage by forgiving your spouse.

You may find that some rocks are easier to drop than others. For instance, dealing with your spouse's hurtful remarks about your appearance, or forgiving her blowing the budget on something unnecessary are irritating but not as serious as an affair, no lovemaking, destructive communication patterns, and so on. The more serious issues will take more effort and perhaps even professional intervention to overcome and let go. Be willing to seek professional help, especially if there are safety issues involved.

On this date, deal with the small rocks in your hand. You can let them go by forgiving your spouse and giving your spouse a clean slate.

CHOOSE TO FORGIVE

Forgiveness begins with a choice, an act of the will. It is not dependent on your spouse asking for forgiveness or even acknowledging the wrong he or she has done. Are you willing to let the rock go? This means not bringing it up again. Remember, forgiving is not forgetting, but slowly the memory of the hurt will fade. Then you know it's really in the past.

In the meantime, take pride in how far you've journeyed toward improving your relationship. Surviving marital strife with your relationship intact can only increase your potential for a loving, fulfilling marriage. Forgiveness is the oil that lubricates a love relationship. It can also heal the burns from the previous hot rocks you held on to.

Once you have forgiven your spouse, how can you move on and not pick up the hot rock again? One suggestion we often make is to plan ahead by making a list of the positive things your spouse has done that make you feel good. The next time you sense irritation rising about something you've forgiven and let go of, try replacing your negative thoughts with something more positive from your list. The more light you shine on the positive memories the sooner the negative memories will fade back into the darkness.

When Forgiveness Comes Second

If you are a victim of domestic violence, forgiveness may be something you need to work on eventually, but your first task is to get help. Forgiveness does not mean putting yourself or your loved ones in danger. Domestic violence, chronic adultery, and child molestation are just a few examples that come to mind. While it is important for your own sake to forgive eventually so you can drop the hot rock of abuse and move on with your life, forgiveness does not mean tolerating threats to your physical or emotional wellbeing.

WHEN YOU NEED FORGIVENESS

And what about the times you are the one needing forgiveness? How hard or easy is it for you to ask for forgiveness? Asking for and giving forgiveness is vital to our mental health. We know a director of a mental hospital who said that half of his patients would be able to go home if they were forgiven and knew they were forgiven. Do you find that as motivating as we do?

If you need to ask for forgiveness, do it in the appropriate way. Focus on what you have done wrong, not on your spouse's shortcomings. To say, "I'm sorry. I was wrong. Please forgive me," can be one of the most healing things that you can say to your partner. For example, "Honey, I'm sorry. I was wrong to nag you about the time you spend on your notebook. Will you forgive me?" Not:

"I'm sorry I nagged you about always being on your notebook, but you're spending too much time on it and ignoring me. It's like you're addicted." Remember to focus on your inappropriate response. Don't use this moment as an opportunity to attack your spouse. If you attack your partner, you're attacking your own marriage team.

We encourage you to forgive and to ask for forgiveness. Your marriage will be stronger and you will experience a deeper, more personal spiritual connection. Along with the core values of unconditional love and acceptance and forgiveness, next let's look at the core value of prayer.

Prayer

Another core belief and touch point for connecting your faith and your love is the discipline of prayer. Prayer is a unique spiritual resource in marriage. Praying together promotes spiritual closeness, but it hasn't always been easy for us to do. In fact, for years, we didn't pray together. I (Dave) am the one who dragged my feet. I knew praying together would be a good thing to do, but just the thought of it was threatening to me. I didn't feel secure in verbalizing my thoughts. Claudia was always more verbal and praying out loud came more naturally to her. Finally, Claudia wore me down, and I agreed to try it. At first it was a real disaster. Claudia would start praying. She'd pray about this and pray about that. All the while, I was thinking, "What can I pray about?" Before I knew it, Claudia had covered my concerns as well. So when she finally stropped praying, the only thing I could think of to say was, "Amen."

She looked at me with disappointment, and asked, "Why didn't you pray too?"

"You covered it all," I told her. This was *not* a marriage builder.

So we stopped even trying to pray together until a friend gave us this tip: "Before you pray together, together make a list of things you want to pray about. Then take turns praying through the list." What great advice that was! Today we don't always make lists, but sometimes we still do. Another thing that has enriched our prayer life is praying together when we're hiking or even driving in the car. Here are a few other ideas from couples who have mastered the art of praying together:

- Pray silently together.
- Hold hands as you pray together.
- Read a prayer.
- Pray the words of a hymn. (Many hymns make beautifully worded prayers.)
- Pray together before you go to bed at night.

If you're looking for a simple way to begin, take this tip from our Quaker friends and try the spiritual practice of sharing silence. This allows you to pray according to your own personal needs, to seek communion with God individually and privately, and yet still be supported by the awareness that your spouse is also sharing in the experience. It's an easy first step in praying together. According to the Quaker tradition, the devotional time is appropriately concluded with the kiss of peace.[6]

Along with praying together, we also encourage you to develop the habit of having devotions together. We like to call them "spiritual discovery times." If you want to start right away, pick up our book *10 Great Dates: Connecting Faith, Love and Marriage.* Consider it "devotional lite" with a fun dating element. It's definitely nonthreatening and easy to do!

Prayer enriches our relationship. We were amazed to read that 81 percent of happy couples reported praying frequently or extensively as a means of addressing marital problems. "Praying together helps to deescalate conflict and enhances cooperative goals and forgiveness."[7] Another core value that brings us closer together is serving others together.

Note from a Dating Couple

At times when we don't see things eye to eye and get into disagreements, our faith is a source of help. Sometimes I give in and accept my husband's point of view; other times he's the one who gives in to me. It helps to pray together and we really believe our faith connection makes a difference.

Service

Mutual service is a core value in most spiritually connected marriages. We believe our shared life must have a sacrificial quality, which leads to service. First we try to serve each other. Then we try to serve others.

We never have functioned very well in our marriage when one or the other has to travel. It was especially hard when our children were small and Dave traveled a lot. He would come home exhausted and tired of being with people. One time he had worked for months designing a computer system for a company and went on a trip that was to close the deal. At the last minute the company's president reneged on the agreement. All Dave's hard work was lost, and he came home empty-handed. No signed contract! He was discouraged, ready to jump into his shell and hibernate.

What was Claudia doing during this time? She was home with a one-year-old and a three-year-old. The older child had just shared his chicken pox with his baby brother. Claudia had been homebound and was itching to get out of the house and have some adult conversation. She was ready for reinforcements and couldn't wait for Dave to get home and help! Needless to say, neither of us was in any mood to serve the other.

Claudia couldn't understand why Dave couldn't be more sensitive to her needs, and Dave just wanted to be by himself. We exchanged heated words accusing each other of being selfish. After being miserable as long as we could stand it, we apologized and started over again. Years later, we still get caught up in the web of "my" needs and "your" needs. We still have to apologize and start over. Knowing the principle doesn't mean that we always apply it. But it is our goal to do so.

Think of ways you can serve each other—like being sensitive to your mate's mood. If Claudia had not crowded Dave when he came home discouraged from that business trip, things might have gone differently. Consider if you might be willing to give up what you want to do and defer to your spouse. Dave, before retreating, could have gone the extra mile and offered to watch the chicken pox kids so Claudia could have a breather.

As part of our faith we are committed to serving others as well as serving each other. When we acknowledge that our life together is part of a larger divine purpose, we look for ways to live out our faith in service to others. Can you think of ways you can serve others together? Maybe you are concerned about ecology and taking better care of our world. Or perhaps you would like to help Habitat for Humanity build houses for people who need a place to live. Your own place of worship offers many opportunities for service. For those who desire to serve, you don't have to look very far to find those who desperately need your help! Every time we get involved in serving others together, our own marriage seems to benefit.

Note from a Dating Couple

Last Christmas we decided to call up a few families, go to an assisted living home, and put on a little nativity play and sing songs. It was so much fun and brought our family so much closer together. We stopped worrying about our wants and focused on helping someone else. It brought such a happy spirit into our home.

Connecting Your Faith and Love

Are you ready to take the next step, to examine your core beliefs and values, to love unconditionally and accept each other, to forgive, pray, and serve one another and others together? Then you're well on your way to having a shared purpose in life — a calling to something greater than the two of you. Our faith sees us through life's storms and gives us inner peace in the midst of a turbulent world. We are convinced that having spiritual intimacy in marriage increases marital satisfaction.

Perhaps you're facing a life storm — an illness, a financial stress, a job loss, or a broken relationship. Everyone has problems in at least one of these areas. Whatever fears and crises you are presently facing now is the time to affirm those things that are truly important in life.

Thousands of years ago, King Solomon saw the value of spiritual intimacy when he said that two are better than one, because they have a good return for their work.... But even better, a cord of three strands is not quickly broken.[8]

Our relationship works best when we acknowledge that our marriage cord has three strands. What are those three strands? Dave is one strand. Claudia is another. The third strand is the spiritual dimension of our marriage. We see our marriage as a partnership with each other and with God. Many times we let each other down, and it's then that we look to the third strand to keep our cord strong, to hold us together when our individual strands are frayed. Our spiritual connection also allows us to take risks, to step out of our comfort zone, and to grow closer to God and to each other.

Let us encourage you to accept the challenge to develop a shared core-belief system. Be willing to open yourself up to your spouse and make yourself vulnerable. And remember to use the communication skills you learned in Dates Two and Three, which will help you to handle each other's feelings with great care. Even if you are not on the same page spiritually, this date can bring you closer. Your marriage will benefit.

Now turn to Date Nine in the Dating Guide
and continue your journey together.

Achieving an Intentional MARRIAGE

One of the favorite parts of our Marriage Alive seminar is the last session when we talk about having an intentional marriage. We give couples time to talk together about what they want for their marriage in the future. We stress the importance of being on the same page about how much they want their lives to overlap (time together, shared activities, and so on) and what is realistic at this stage of their life. After they brainstorm together and make a list of potential goals for their marriage, we have them choose one, two, or at the most three goals they agree to work on in the coming weeks and months.

We emphasize realistic and achievable goals. Once these first goals are achieved, they can move on to the others. Each couple then writes their chosen goals on their personal *"Declaration of Intention"* as an official document of the commitment they make to pursue an intentional marriage. And this is just what you'll get to do on this date.

In a recent seminar Caitlyn and Josh shared their *Declaration of Intention* with us. They had two goals. The first was, "We want to dream together again."

"I told Josh that what I really wanted was for us to dream together again like we did in the early years of our marriage," Caitlyn explained. "I don't even care if we can't fulfill all our dreams — it's the 'dreaming together' process that's really important to me."

"That's important to me too," Josh added, "but what I'm really excited about is the second goal — to do some financial planning together. I also like it that you told us to choose only a couple of goals to start with and to make sure they are practical, measurable, believable goals. In the past when we've attended seminars like this, I've left frustrated and sometimes even angry because there was no way I could do everything I had been challenged to do. But now I'm going home encouraged because we can make these two goals happen."

You can make your goals happen too, and now is the time to nail down just what you want those goals to be, and how you can have an intentional marriage. Just as you had to set aside time for each of your dates, you need to be intentional going forward about continuing to grow together. If you're committed and realistic, by the end of this date you will have your very own blueprint for an intentional marriage — one that is believable, practical, measureable, fun, and easy-to-follow.

Note from a Dating Couple

This seminar provided the focused time we needed to think intentionally about our marriage and how to improve it. Plus we now have tools we can use to build our marriage.

First, we'll look at three degrees of marriage involvement (how much you want your circles to overlap) and help you determine which best fits your life right now. Then we'll guide you through the process of setting realistic goals and developing your strategy for achieving them. Finally, you'll have the opportunity to write and sign your own *Declaration of Intention*. The key to having an intentional marriage is designing a custom plan that is realistic and doable for you.

Three Degrees of Marriage Involvement

How involved are you with your spouse? To help you set realistic goals, you need to consider the constraints of your present season of life and how much overlapping of your lives is realistic. Consider the three degrees of involvement illustrated below: minimum, moderate, and maximum.[1]

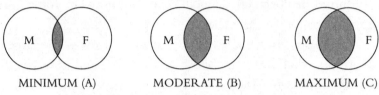

MINIMUM (A)   MODERATE (B)   MAXIMUM (C)

DEGREES OF INVOLVEMENT IN MARRIAGE

The degree to which the circles overlap is not as important as agreeing with each other about where you are right now and where you would like to be in the future. To better understand the degrees of involvement, let's take a closer look at what each image represents.

MINIMUM INVOLVEMENT

In a minimum-involvement marriage, your circles overlap very little. Perhaps both of you are in full-time, high-stress jobs. Or one spouse has a heavy travel schedule while the other spouse balances responsibilities with home, kids, and other life-management tasks. You might text message each other during the day and most evenings carve out a few minutes for a video chat, but it's not the same as actually being together.

When we were first married and in the military, Dave was at a missile battery and on duty practically every other night. Claudia taught in the US Army educational program for GIs who were trying to complete high school. As much as we wanted our circles to overlap, there was very little time to make that happen. Back then we didn't have FaceTime, instant messaging, email, or even mobile phones. When we were apart, we were really apart, except for the occasional phone call.

MODERATE INVOLVEMENT

For the active parenting years, we were in the moderate involvement style. (We've experienced all of them at some point in our marriage.)

Some couples, like Mike and Leah, have to work really hard to maintain a moderate level while managing separate careers. When Mike had the opportunity to go into business for himself, he and Leah spent many days and hours talking through the implications for their marriage and family. (They have two young children.) Together, they decided to go for it.

Mike's hours are long, and he spends most weekends finishing urgent projects. Leah's job is not so stressful, though, and neither of them has a job that requires travel. Still, it's a real challenge to make their circles overlap. Rather than complain, they look for ways to work together to accomplish projects at home. For instance, together they carved out time to paint their bedroom. They love to garden together and recently built a fence in the backyard so that their kids could safely play outside as they worked in the yard.

For Mike and Leah, it's hard enough to stay in the moderate involvement zone. The maximum level is unrealistic for them, and the minimum level is below their expectations for their marriage. Most couples tend to fall somewhere in the moderate involvement range.

MAXIMUM INVOLVEMENT

At this point in our lives, our circles overlap quite a bit. We lead seminars and training conferences together; we write together; and we even have desks that face each other! (I know you're probably thinking, "That just goes too far!" And for many couples, you'd be right!) We have common interests and mutual friends, and when we have the opportunity, we absolutely love hiking together.

We still have interests and activities that do not include the other, but we actually have to work on having a little separateness in our relationship. It's easy to have too much togetherness. Recently, I (Claudia) was working at my favorite spot in the kitchen updating a chapter in this book and was deep in thought—in the zone—no interruptions please. In walked David and shared a light-hearted comment about something that at that particular moment I frankly didn't care about or want to hear. So I politely (or not so politely) told him, "Go away!"

Of course, you can still have a maximum-involvement relationship without working together. Perhaps you call, text, or FaceTime five or six times a day to check in or consult on a decision, or your interests and friends are virtually identical—this also qualifies.

WHAT'S YOUR DEGREE OF INVOLVEMENT?

How would you describe your marriage? After going through the previous nine dates, do your circles overlap more than they did before the dates? Do the two of you agree on the assessment of your present degree of involvement?[2]

The next step is to talk about the degree of involvement you both would like to have. Compromise may be part of the process. Remember to use the connecting style of communication and express how you feel without attacking the other or defending yourself. You may want to talk about things you would like to do together and things you would like to do separately.

After identifying where you want to be, you can begin to set realistic goals to help you get there.

Set Realistic Goals

Our challenge to you is the same challenge we gave to Caitlyn and Josh. On this date we want you to brainstorm together and make a list of what you want for your marriage. You might want to look back through the previous nine dates and make a robust list of possible goals. Basically, a marriage goal is a target toward which you agree to work. Once you have set goals, you can then set objectives—specific, measurable steps you can take to reach your goals.

Here are some examples of goals to jumpstart your thinking:

- To reclaim and redo our bedroom to make it more conducive for relaxing and loving each other. (We will inform the kids that this is now our private place!)
- To have a "couple's business meeting" each week where we can talk about issues we need to discuss and practice using our newly acquired communication skills.

- To become more united and responsible in our finances and develop a realistic budget.
- To choose a project to do together, something to learn together, or do a service project to complete for someone else.
- To start the tradition of a weekly date night.

Obviously you can't work on all the goals on your list at the same time, so the next step is to choose one or two goals to focus on for the next few weeks or months. We suggest starting with a goal in which you can quickly see some progress, like choosing a weekly date night. Then, as you are encouraged by your success, you can build on it by tackling some of your more complex or long-term goals.

Another option is to pick two goals. One goal is an "us" goal you both agree on that will take both of you working on it to complete it. The second goal is an "I" goal that will benefit the marriage, but is 100 percent dependent on the individual to complete.

USE FIVE QUESTIONS TO GET YOU STARTED

Let five questions guide you as you choose your goals and devise a plan of action. First ask, *What? Why? How? When?* After tackling those four questions, you'll greatly increase your odds of success by answering one more: *What could stop us from achieving our goal?* A quick overview of all five questions follows, and to help you see how they work we've incorporated how one couple worked through this process to identify their goals and to create a plan of action to achieve them.

What? What is the marriage goal you have chosen? Define your goal as specifically as possible so you're both clear and on the same page. For example, develop a financial plan with a realistic budget or plan a weekend getaway without the children.

Why? What is your motivation for setting this goal? How will achieving this goal move your marriage forward? Understanding the "why" increases your chances of success and will motivate you to take the time and make the effort to create and accomplish this goal.

How? The next question is, "How are we going to reach this goal?" The answer to this question needs to be specific, achievable, and measurable so you will know when you get there. Write down the actions steps you agree to take that will help you accomplish your goal. (You could look at the these specific steps as "baby step goals.")

When? If you fail to answer this question, you will not reach your goal. Why? Because having a firm date requires commitment. So get out your calendars and block the time you need to accomplish your action items. For instance, if you set a goal to have a date night each week for the next four weeks, block out the next four Friday nights as date night. Then, commit yourselves to following your plan.

What could stop us from achieving our goal? This question helps you think through potential obstacles and put plans in place to address them. If you are proactive and anticipate problems, your chances of success go way up. For example, what will you do when you or your spouse fall short of your goal? If you practice the forgiveness you learned in Date Nine and then persist in making your goal happen, you can still achieve your goals.

Jeremy and Tiffany, a couple in one of our seminars, wanted to keep working on connecting so they chose two goals: to have a weekly date night and to work on their communication. Here is their plan of action using the five questions to help them reach their communication goal:

What? We want to improve our communication and nail down the communication skills we've learned on our dates.

Why? Sharpening our communication skills will help us connect and bring us closer together. And we'll be able to do a better job of discussing problems when they arise.

How? Here are the steps we plan to take to upgrade our communication.

- We will take ten minutes each evening before we go to bed to check in with each other. We will carve out time each week to have a date away from home so we can talk without interruptions.
- We will choose a blog or podcast on communication to read or listen or watch together.

- We will go online and choose an e-book to download and read.
- We'll have a weekly thirty-minute couple time when we can talk about issues and practice using the feelings formula and speaker/listener technique.

When? Here are the times we have chosen to work on our communication:

- Friday night will be our default date night, but if there's a conflict we'll have our date on Saturday or Sunday.
- On Wednesday evenings we will set aside thirty minutes to talk about any issues we need to address.
- We will add these times to our calendars and try to protect them from interruptions.
- During the week we will look for other small bits of time to talk with each other.

What could stop us from achieving our goal? Things that might stop us from achieving our goal include:

- Unexpected changes of plans that are out of our control.
- Underestimating the time this will take.
- Getting discouraged if we don't follow through with each commitment.

Realistically, Jeremy and Tiffany knew their best-laid plans could still get derailed. But just anticipating how they might respond to interruptions and roadblocks gave them courage to move forward with their action plan. They agreed that when they encountered obstacles they would together find a way through or around them.

For Couples Separated by Military Service

If one or both of you serve in the military, perhaps you're thinking, "But you don't understand our situation!" You're right, we don't. Our hearts and prayers go out to you. You are our heroes! We recently did a Skype interview to encourage military couples who are in incredibly difficult situations. We shared with them how couples stationed at Fort Bragg, North Carolina, have found time to date—even when they are separated by deployment.

To help couples facing a separation due to deployment, Fort Bragg offered (for free) the first five dates in this book to help couples prepare for the separation. When they returned, they offered the last five dates to help them readjust to being together again. They gave some of the couples two copies of 10 Great Dates—one copy to the spouse being deployed and another to the spouse left behind. Then they arranged video conferencing dates through Skype. It's amazing what you can achieve, even in very stressful situations.

MONITOR YOUR PROGRESS

As they work on their goals, Jeremy and Tiffany will need to monitor their progress closely. The research is clear. Your chances of achieving your goals increases significantly when you write them down and track your progress.

What about those pesky interruptions and obstacles? You can be sure they will appear. That's why it's so it's important to monitor your progress and be willing to flex when things don't go as planned. Some weeks your time together won't happen. Kids get sick, an unexpected project deadline must be met, drop-in guests appear, or other unforeseeable things happen. But even if you don't follow through with every activity, you will still be closer to reaching your goal than if you had not planned at all. So be realistic, but also persevere.

Perhaps most importantly, be gentle with yourself and each other when you fall short. The research is also clear that contrary to popular opinion, those who are compassionate and gentle with themselves and their spouses are much more likely to achieve their goals than those who are hard on themselves and their spouses.

Love Grows through the Little Things

Whatever challenges you face, look for time in little places. We love the German language title of our new book, Liebe Lebt von Kleinen Zeichen. Here's a loose translation, "Love grows through the little things." What "little things" can you do today to invest in your marriage? Send a text? Leave a voice message? Write a Post-it note? Give a ten-second kiss and twenty-second hug? Say, "I love you?" Take the little bits of time you have and invest them today. You can have an intentional marriage!

Will 10 Great Dates Make a Difference?

We started the chapter with Josh and Caitlyn's story, and now we want to conclude by sharing one more story of a couple who had their marriage restored through experiencing their *10 Great Dates*. Julie and Mike were headed for divorce, but they still wanted to save their marriage and restore their relationship. Here is how Julie describes their story:

• • •

My husband, Mike, and I had been separated for over a year and I believed divorce was our only option. We decided to give it one more try and went for counseling. At our counselor's suggestion, we did 10 Great Dates.

For our first date, we both dressed up (just as you suggest). We agreed to focus on the content of Date One and not to talk about our children, marriage problems, and so on.

We went to a nice restaurant, ordered, and nervously got out our dating exercise. Amazingly, as we started going down memory lane, something immediately sparked between us! We had so much fun sharing our answers and remembering our lives together nineteen years ago. I was amazed at how much Mike remembered about our dating and about our wedding day. Talking about the day we met made us both cry.

I had agreed to go with Mike on a business trip to Las Vegas the following week. I was apprehensive about going, but after our first date, I actually started to look forward to it. We both felt like a young couple going off together for the first time.

The week was more wonderful than we ever dreamed it could be. In fact, it was better than our honeymoon! One evening as we were walking hand in hand, I got tingly all over. I looked over at Mike and realized I still loved him very much. It was like falling in love again, and the best part was that this man already knew me and all my faults, and he was the father of my children to boot! I shared my thoughts with him, and that was a turning point for us. Through 10 Great Dates *we learned how to trust each other and share more deeply with each other. Two months later, my girls and I moved back home. It was like we were never gone.*

I have to say, 10 Great Dates *did more for our marriage than counseling did, and we thank you from the bottom of our hearts.*

Julie and Mike

• • •

From time to time over the years, we often thought about Julie and Mike and wondered how they were doing—if they were still together and if what they learned initially through *10 Great Dates* had helped them not only to rebuild their relationship but to have a truly enriched and intentional marriage. Six years later, Julie sent us a copy of a letter she had just written to the editor at a Denver newspaper that describes their subsequent journey.

• • •

My husband and I beat the odds of couples separating and not surviving. We were separated for sixteen months and planned to divorce, but through faith, prayer, friends and a wonderful program called 10 Great Dates, *we remembered why and how we fell in love, now twenty-six years ago.*

After six years of being back together, Mike has not disappointed me. Don't get me wrong, we are human and we still have arguments, but we have learned a lot from 10 Great Dates *and from counselors and other courses we attended at church. We now know that it is more important to communicate, have time out instead of "blowing up" if a problem is not resolving or going our way, and not to let the sun go down on our anger. Mike and I have learned that it doesn't matter who says "I'm sorry" first—but it sure opens the door for forgiveness. When you truly love someone, being right all the time isn't what is important. Letting that person know you love and cherish them is what is important. Mike does that for me each and every day, and I share it back with him.*

Mike and I have always felt called to share our story when the opportunity arises. We hope it will help at least one person or couple striving to save their marriage.

Julie and Mike

• • •

We're so grateful to Julie and Mike for sharing their story. We hope their story will encourage you that no matter how challenging your circumstances may be, you too can build a loving and intentional marriage.

Time to Celebrate!

Like Julie and Mike, you've made it all the way to Date Ten and it's time to celebrate. It's been quite the journey, and we commend you for your desire to build a strong and intimate marriage through experiencing *10 Great Dates*. We hope that by now dating has become a habit.

Over your dates you've had the opportunity to connect on a more personal level and to learn how to use anger and conflict to energize your marriage and to manage problems in a more positive way. We hope you have become better friends and have a deeper love and appreciation for each other—that you have infused your relationship with intimacy, fun, and romance. We challenge you to keep dating and celebrating your marriage. Use this last date to craft your own blueprint for achieving an intentional marriage. And always, remember to have fun along the way! Happy dating!

Keep Dating!

Keep your dating momentum going and download our bonus Mystery Great Date at www.10GreatDates.org. While you are there, you can also sign up for our Great Dates blog and updates.

Now, your final date awaits! Turn to Date Ten and get ready to develop a great plan for continuing your intentional marriage.

Postscript

Congratulations! You have completed *10 Great Dates!* We hope dating has given you a deeper love for and understanding of your spouse and helped to make your marriage a high priority. But the challenge of having an intentional marriage is ongoing. So where do you go from here? Now comes the responsibility to continue in the things you have learned and to pass them on to other couples.

Many marriages today are functioning far below their potential. But you can do something about it—your marriage can light the way for others. We need a widespread movement of couples choosing to prioritize their marriage, to date their mate, and to encourage other couples to do the same.

One of the great benefits of our work in marriage education over the years is that it has motivated us to continue working on our own marriage. As you have probably gleaned from the pages of this book, our marriage is still a work in process. Please do not consider your *10 Great Dates* a one-time experience. We know couples who repeat *10 Great Dates* each year as an annual marriage check-up.

As we continue to work on our own marriage, we encourage you to do the same. And it really helps to have supportive friends who gently nudge you to grow your marriage. If you start a fire with only one log, the flame may go dim, but several logs together burn brightly. To keep the fires of your marriage burning brightly, consider starting your own *10 Great Dates* group. Simply invite a few other couples to join you in your home, or start a group in your church or community. It's a fun program that is easy to lead, guy-friendly, and skill-based. Couples come for great dates and go home with marriage skills. The bar is low and the benefits are high. It's a great way to pass on what you've learned from your own great dates.

This book can be your guide. Other Great Dates resources, including video date launches for this book, are available at www.10greatdates .org. You can also leave your feedback and comments at our website. In the meantime, keep dating and having fun together!

Notes

DATE TWO: Learning to Communicate

1. Staff, "Talk? Send a Text, Dear: One in Ten Couples Only Chat by Email or Phone," *DailyMail.com* (October 5, 2010), http://www.dailymail.co.uk/news/article–1318049/1–10-couples-talk-email-text-mobile-phone-calls.html.

2. Brandon T. McDaniel and Sarah M. Coyne, " 'Technoference': The Interface of Technology in Couple Relationships and Implications for Women's Personal and Relational Well-Being," *Psychology of Popular Media Culture* (2014).

3. We learned the concept of the feelings formula from Bill and Kathy Clarke, who led Marriage and Family Enrichment Institutes. We met the Clarkes when we were just beginning our work in marriage enrichment, and their input over the years has enriched our lives and our work.

4. Peter Hartley, *Interpersonal Communication*, 2nd ed. (New York: Routledge, 1999), 10.

DATE THREE: Solving Problems as a Couple

1. John Gottman, "The Scientific Basis for The Orcas Island Couples' Retreat: Some of the Basic Research Findings," Gottman Private Couples' Retreats (accessed October 15, 2015), http://www.gottmancouplesretreats.com/about/relationships-research-conflict-friendship-meaning.aspx.

2. We thank Doug Wilson for sharing his illustration of animal characters with us in Vienna, Austria, in 1981 and giving us

permission to adapt his concept for use in our work in marriage enrichment. Doug and his wife, Karen, spent several days with us when we were first designing our Marriage Alive seminar and gave strategic input that has benefited us and many other couples through the years. http://douglasawilson.com.

3. Michele Weiner-Davis, "The Walkaway Wife Syndrome," *Michele's Articles* (blog), *Divorce Busting: Michele Weiner-Davis* (2009), http://divorcebusting.com/a_walkaway_wife.htm.

4. Howard Markman, Scott Stanley, and Susan L. Blumberg, *Fighting for Your Marriage* (San Francisco: Jossey-Bass, 1994), 76. Drs. Markman, Stanley, and Blumberg are marital researchers and founders of PREP™ (The Prevention and Relationship Enhancement Program). PREP is a research-based approach to teaching couples how to communicate effectively, work as a team to solve problems, manage conflicts without damaging closeness, and preserve and enhance commitment and friendship. The PREP approach is based on over thirty years of research in the field of marital health and success, with much of the specific research conducted at the University of Denver over the past fifteen years. For more information about PREP, go to PREPINC.com or call 1–303–759–9931.

5. See Ephesians 4:26.

6. Adapted from David Mace, *Love and Anger in Marriage* (Grand Rapids: Zondervan, 1982), 109–12. Our basic philosophy of how to deal with anger and conflict is adapted from our training with our mentors, David and Vera Mace, used with their permission.

7. Markmman et al., *Fighting for Your Marriage*, 110-12. Used by permission. To order *Fighting for Your Marriage* books or audio or video resources, call 800-366-0166. Copyright by PREP Educational Products, Inc., 1991, http://www.prepinc.com.

8. See http://www.goodreads.com/quotes/144557-resentment-is-like-drinking-poison-and-then-hoping-it-will.

9. Linda Waite and Maggie Gallagher, *The Case for Marriage: Why Married People are Happier, Healthier and Better Off Financially* (New York: Broadway, 2001).

DATE FOUR: Becoming an Encourager

1. Kashmir Hill, "Facebook Manipulated 689,003 Users' Emotions for Science," *Tech* (blog), *Forbes* (June 28, 2014), http://www.forbes.com/sites/kashmirhill/2014/06/28/facebook-manipulated—689003-users-emotions-for-science/.

2. John Gottman, PhD, *Why Marriages Succeed or Fail* (New York: Simon & Schuster, 1994), 29.

DATE FIVE: Finding Unity in Our Diversity

1. Scott Barry Kauffman, "Will the Real Introverts Please Stand Up?" *Beautiful Minds* (blog), *Scientific American* (June 9, 2014), http://blogs.scientificamerican.com/beautiful-minds/will-the-real-introverts-please-stand-up/.

DATE SIX: Building a Creative Love Life!

1. "Idea of a Perfect Evening," *Ladies Home Journal* (November 1994), 52.

2. For those caught in the pornography web, it is possible to rewire the brain for a normal sexual response cycle. Those who are struggling with this issue would be wise to seek out the help of an experienced professional counselor.

3. David Arp and Claudia Arp, *Love Life for Parents* (Grand Rapids: Zondervan, 1998), 68.

4. 1 Peter 4:8.

5. Proverbs 24:26.

6. This exercise was developed years ago by Masters and Johnson to help couples who were experiencing problems in their sexual relationship. One interesting "side effect" they discovered was the vast majority of couples who tried this technique reported a significant increase in desire, or that "loving feeling."

7. For additional guidance on the Sensate-Focus Exercise, see our book *Fighting for Your Empty Nest Marriage: Reinventing Your Relationship When the Kids Leave Home,* Jossey-Bass Psychology Series

(San Francisco: Jossey-Bass, 2001), 279–80. You can also Google "Sensate-Focus Technique."

8. Judith S. Wallerstein and Sandra Blakeslee, *The Good Marriage: How and Why Love Lasts* (New York: Warner, 1996), 192.

9. Esther Perel, "The Secret to Desire in a Long-Term Relationship" (filmed February 2013), TEDSalon NY2013, http://www.ted.com/talks/esther_perel_the_secret_to_desire_in_a_long_term_relationship?language=en.

10. Yagana Shah, "Married Couples' Sex Lives Rebound—After 50 Years, Study Finds," *Post50*, *Huffington Post* (February 2, 2015), http://www.huffingtonpost.com/2015/02/19/married-couples-sex-lives-rebound-study_n_6713126.html.

DATE SEVEN: Sharing Responsibility and Working Together

1. If money is an area of struggle for you, you might want to check out Dave Ramsey's website at www.daveramsey.com. He has some awesome budgeting and money tips. http://www.daveramsey.com/blog/3-ways-to-get-spouse-on-board-financially.

2. Daniel Goleman, *Emotional Intelligence: Why It Can Matter More than IQ* (New York: Bantam, 1995).

DATE EIGHT: Balancing Your Dual Role As Partner and Parent

1. Abraham Maslow, *Motivation and Personality* (New York: Worth, 1970).

DATE NINE: Connecting Faith, Love, and Marriage

1. Les and Leslie Parrott, *Saving Your Marriage Before It Starts* (Grand Rapids: Zondervan, 1995), 145.

2. Ed Stetzer, "Marriage, Divorce and the Church: What Do the Stats Say, and Can Marriage Be Happy?" *The Exchange* (blog), *Christianity Today* (February 14, 2014), http://www.christianitytoday.com/edstetzer/2014/february/marriage-divorce-and-body-of-christ-what-do-stats-say-and-c.html.

3. Parrott and Parrott, *Saving Your Marriage Before It Starts*, 135.

4. 1 Corinthians 13:4–5.

5. Howard Markman, Scott Stanley, and Susan L. Blumberg, *Fighting for Your Marriage* (San Francisco: Jossey-Bass, 1994), 285.

6. David and Claudia Arp, *The Second Half of Marriage: Facing the Eight Challenges of the Empty-Nest Years* (Grand Rapids: Zondervan, 1996), 64–67.

7. Mark H. Butler, Julie A. Stout, and Brandt C. Gardner, "Prayer as a Conflict Resolution Ritual: Clinical Implications of Religious Couples' Report of Relationship Softening, Healing Perspective, and Change Responsibility," *The American Journal of Family Therapy* 30, no 1 (2002), 19–37.

8. Ecclesiastes 4:9–12.

DATE TEN: Achieving an Intentional Marriage

1. David and Vera Mace, *We Can Have Better Marriages if We Really Want Them* (Nashville: Abingdon, 1974), 76.

DATE SIX EXERCISE

1. The original idea of this exercise came from our friend Kathy Clarke.

10 Bonus Great Dates

BONUS DATE 1: MARRIAGE HISTORY

Spend an evening looking through old pictures, videos, and scrapbooks together. One couple saved all the cards (birthday, anniversary, etc.) they had sent to each other over the years and had a great date reading through them and remembering their good times together.

BONUS DATE 2: THE OUT-OF-TOWNERS

Drive to the next town so you won't bump into people you know and choose a quiet restaurant for a low-key dinner full of conversation.

BONUS DATE 3: RECONNECTING

Pull out your old family scrapbooks and videos. Look at and talk about pictures of your families of origin—your parents and grandparents, aunts and uncles. See how many pictures of relatives you can find and talk about which ones influenced your lives.

BONUS DATE 4: MOVIE NIGHTS

Separately, pick out a movie of your choice. Then compare. How different are your choices? Plan two dates, one to watch your movie of choice and another to watch your partner's movie of choice.

BONUS DATE 5: TAKE-A-HIKE

Pack a picnic lunch in your backpack and take a day hike. It's amazing how much easier it is to talk with your partner as you hike together.

BONUS DATE 6: HAVE A COZY TALK

Spend a cozy evening at home in front of the fire, in a candlelit room, or on your patio or deck. Talk about all the things that are good about your relationship that you want to continue to nurture in the future.

BONUS DATE 7: BUCKET LIST

Make your own bucket list. Dream about the experiences you would like to have, places you would like to go, or challenges you would like to surmount together. Prioritize your list and talk about what might actually be possible. What would you do and where would you go if money were no object? It's okay to dream together!

BONUS DATE 8: THE DREAM GETAWAY

Spend some time together with a mobile device at a local coffee shop to do additional research on the details, logistics, and costs of your dream getaway. Take your plans as far as you can, but don't book it till you have the resources. Just enjoy the process of dreaming and planning together.

BONUS DATE 9: SOUL MATE FORGIVENESS

Visit a place of worship that is open to the public for prayer and meditation. Sit in a pew or kneel together at the altar. If you need to, ask each other for forgiveness for past hurts and give each other the gift of a blank slate. Recommit yourself to the core beliefs that help you connect your faith, love, and marriage.

BONUS DATE 10: NEW HORIZONS

Attend a marriage enrichment workshop, seminar, or retreat where you have an extended time to enjoy being together and focusing on each other.

10 GREAT D♡TES®

If you've enjoyed your Great Dates, here are some ways you can help us share them with others.

- Recommend this book to your Facebook friends; Tweet about them; Pin on Pinterest or any other social media; or mention in your blog post.

- Write a review on Amazon.com, BN.com, CBD.com, and goodreads.com.

- Suggest 10 Great Dates to your small group, church, and community groups. (Check out video curriculum at 10greatdates.org.)

- Give to friends and family as a wedding, anniversary, or birthday present with money for their first Great Date.

- Suggest the Arps to your church or group for a Marriage Alive Seminar or Great Date Night. For information on how to bring Claudia and David to your church and community, email 10GreatDates@gmail.com.

- Get trained as a 10 Great Dates trainer. For more information, email 10GreatDates@gmail.com.

- Send us your great date ideas and tips at 10GreatDates@gmail.com. We just love getting "Notes from Dating Couples"!

*Subscribe to our Great Dates Blog at **10GreatDates.org***

10 Great Dates Before Saying I Do

*David and Claudia Arp and
Curt and Natelle Brown*

Here are 10 fun, innovative relationship-building dates for seriously dating and engaged couples!

10 Great Dates Before You Say "I Do" combines the best of marriage preparation research with a fun, easy-to-follow format. Couples will soon discover whether or not to go to the next level of commitment and will spend quality time together now while preparing for a great marriage in the future. Couples will love growing together while going out together.

- Share your hopes and dreams
- Appreciate your differences
- Communicate and connect
- Develop spiritual intimacy
- Evaluate your relationship
- Celebrate romance
- And more!

If you're looking for a unique tool to help you prepare for life-long love, this is it! This creative resource is not simply educational, it's fun!
— Drs. Les & Leslie Parrott, Authors, *Saving
Your Marriage Before It Starts*

Everyone tells couples to get to know each other and to learn to communicate before they get married. This book provides a dating road map that shows the way and makes it fun.
— Diane Sollee, MSW, Director, The
Coalition for Marriage, Family and Couples
Education, L.L.C. SmartMarriages.com

DVD Curriculum available at: *10GreatDates.org*

Available in stores and online!

10 Great Dates for Empty Nesters

David and Claudia Arp

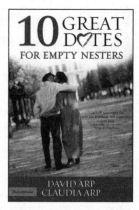

It's just the two of you again, and it's time to renew your relationship. Through ten innovative, fun dates guaranteed to spice up your marriage, you can reconnect and reclaim that same spark, excitement, and creativity that you experienced before you had kids. Specially crafted for empty nesters, these dates are based on marriage-enriching themes, such as

- Becoming a couple again
- Rediscovering intimate talk
- Revitalizing your love life
- Growing together spiritually
- Relating to adult children
- Becoming best friends

10 Great Dates for Empty Nesters offers a simple dating plan that is sure to revive romance and rejuvenate the fun quotient in your empty-nest marriage.

10 Great Dates for Empty Nesters will fill your empty nest with fun, friendship, and romance. It is refreshing to read a book about marriage written by people who don't just believe in marriage, but actually understand how it works.

—John Gray, Author, *Men Are from Mars, Women Are from Venus*

The Second Half of Marriage

Facing the Eight Challenges of the Empty-Nest Years

David and Claudia Arp

Renew your love!
Reinvent your marriage!
Make the rest the best!

Your children are gone or leaving soon. It's time to focus once again on your own future and especially on your marriage. What's in store for the second half? David and Claudia Arp provide answers and practical help in this groundbreaking book. Drawing on their national survey of hundreds of "second-half" couples, the Arps reveal eight marital challenges every long-term marriage faces, and they offer strategies and exercises for meeting each of them.

The Second Half of Marriage will challenge you to create a vision for the rest of your life together—and inspire you to make that vision a reality.

The Second Half of Marriage *is full of rich insights into marriage in later life and the many challenges and hopes it offers. There is great wisdom in this volume in a vital area of life that is too often ignored."*
—John Gottman, Ph.D., marital researcher and author of *Why Marriages Succeed or Fail*

The Arps have blazed the trail to the real "better half" of marriage—and the best is yet to come. Your first step is to get this book. Your second is to take a hike—together!
—Scott Stanley, Ph.D., cofounder PREP and coauthor of *Fighting for Your Marriage*

DVD Curriculum for your small group and personal enjoyment is available at: *10GreatDates.org.*

Available in stores and online!

About Marriage Alive International, Inc.

10 GREAT D♡TES®

Marriage Alive International, Inc., founded by Claudia Arp and David Arp, MSW, is a ground-breaking work dedicated to providing resources, seminars, and training to empower churches, community marriage initiatives, US military, and other groups both nationally and internationally to help build stronger marriages and families. It is the home of the popular *10 Great Dates* marriage education program for which this book is the participant's guide.

This innovative program disguised as "10 great dates" is a low-key, fun, male-friendly, yet skilled-based program that appeals to couples in any setting. The *10 Great Dates* program received the Smart Marriages Impact Award and has been researched by the University of Tennessee and also by a number of initiatives that were funded by federal grants. *10 Great Dates* is also available in Spanish, Korean and German.

Other Marriage Alive DVD-based Curriculum:

- *Great Dates Connect* — Use this shorter 4-date edition with Dates 1, 2, 3, and 5 in this *10 Great Dates* book.

- *Great Dates Before You Say "I Do"* — For seriously dating and engaged couples to help them move forward with confidence and prepare for marriage.

- *The Second Half of Marriage* — Helping couples surmount the 8 challenges of the empty nest years.

> *Claudia and David Arp offer great practical engaging resources for building all the best stuff into your marriage. Let them share their passion for life and relationships with you.*
>
> —Scott Stanley, Ph.D., cofounder of PREP and coauthor of Fighting for Your Marriage

For more information about Marriage Alive go to:
10GreatDates.org

Part Two

YOUR DATING GUIDE

YOUR DATING PLAN

Use the chart below to schedule when you will have each date.

DAY/TIME	DATE
	Date 1: Choosing a High-Priority Marriage
	Date 2: Learning to Communicate
	Date 3: Solving Problems as a Couple
	Date 4: Becoming an Encourager
	Date 5: Finding Unity in Diversity
	Date 6: Building a Creative Love Life
	Date 7: Sharing Responsibility and Working Together
	Date 8: Balancing Your Roles as Partner and Parent
	Date 9: Connecting Faith, Love, and Marriage
	Date 10: Achieving an Intentional Marriage

SMART TIPS FOR GREAT DATES

- Stay positive. This is a great date!
- Talk about your relationship (not your kids, job, or in-laws!).
- Be future focused. Don't bring up past issues.
- If you get on a negative track, stop and get a milkshake with two straws.
- If you get really stuck, ask for help.
- Use good communication skills.
  1. Be honest, yet never unkind.
  2. Start your sentences with "I" and let them reflect back on you.
  3. Resist attacking the other or defending yourself.
  4. Be specific and positive.

Have fun!

Great Dates Exercises

1–10

The exercise pages for the dates that follow
are perforated and can be torn out.

Choosing a High-Priority
MARRIAGE

On Date One you will remember why you got married in the first place and celebrate what's great about your relationship today.

PREPARATION

- Read chapter 1, "Choosing a High-Priority Marriage."

- Read through Date One Exercise and make notes. Looking over the questions before your date gives time for reflection. Plus, if you aren't as verbal as your spouse, writing out a few notes will give you time to formulate your thoughts and lead to more balanced sharing.

- Choose a destination for your date where you can easily talk with each other. If you want to launch your dates at your favorite restaurant, if possible make reservations ahead of time. (The one making the reservations may want to let the place be a surprise.)

- Make any necessary childcare arrangements. If you decide always to have your date on the same day and time each week, consider setting up childcare on a weekly basis for ten weeks.

- Get excited! Treat this like you would have treated one of your first dates together. Remember, this is a date!

DATE NIGHT TIPS

- Before you begin your conversation, review the communication tips in "Smart Tips for Great Dates" (page 160).

- Talk through the exercise one question at a time.

- Use your notes in "Part 1: A Trip Down Memory Lane" to jumpstart your conversation.

- Use your notes in "Part 2: What's Great about Us!" to talk about the present and what is positive about your marriage. Allow enough time for each question and take turns in sharing your answers.

CHAPTER SUMMARY

Choosing to have a high-priority marriage will positively impact your relationship. Life is stressful; work, family, screens, and other activities compete for your time. If you're going to keep your relationship moving forward, you need to be proactive, grab time for each other, and set goals for your marriage. From our own time of crisis in marriage, we chose three goals to help us make our marriage a priority. You can do the same. First, look at and evaluate where your marriage is right now. The second goal is to set goals for the future. The third goal is to learn new relational skills to help your marriage grow. On this date you'll have the opportunity to review your past and look at your marriage as it is today. We suggest also reviewing the three principles for building a successful, high-priority marriage: Put your marriage first, commit to grow together, and work at staying close. You can make your marriage a high priority!

Choosing a High-Priority Marriage

PART 1: A TRIP DOWN MEMORY LANE

Use the questions that follow to reflect on your relationship history and to remember what attracted you to each other in the first place. Note that the two of you will likely remember different things—or remember the same thing differently—and that's okay! Simply sharing your memories together will make a great date.

When was the first time you saw each other? Or did you first meet online?

_____

_____

_____

What was your first date? What did you do? Where did you go?

_____

_____

_____

When did you realize you were connecting with each other in a special way?

_____

_____

_____

What were your favorite times together before you were married?

_____

_____

_____

When was the first time you talked about getting married?

_____

_____

_____

What do you remember most about your wedding day?

_____

_____

_____

What are your best memories from the first year of marriage?

_____

_____

What are your best memories from the past twelve months?

_____

_____

_____

PART 2: WHAT'S GREAT ABOUT US!

1. The three things I'd say are most positive about our relationship right now are:
    1. _____
    2. _____
    3. _____

2. Two things that are fine about our relationship but could be better are:
    1. _____
    2. _____

3. One thing I could do to make our relationship better is:
    1. _____

POST-DATE APPLICATION

- Look for the positives. Find ways to compliment each other between now and the next date.

- Do that one thing you know you can do to make your marriage better.

- Read chapter 2, "Learning to Communicate," and complete the Date Two Exercise.

Choosing a High-Priority Marriage

PART 1: A TRIP DOWN MEMORY LANE

Use the questions that follow to reflect on your relationship history and to remember what attracted you to each other in the first place. Note that the two of you will likely remember different things—or remember the same thing differently—and that's okay! Simply sharing your memories together will make a great date.

When was the first time you saw each other? Or did you first meet online?

_____

_____

_____

What was your first date? What did you do? Where did you go?

_____

_____

_____

When did you realize you were connecting with each other in a special way?

_____

_____

_____

What were your favorite times together before you were married?

_____

_____

_____

When was the first time you talked about getting married?

_____

_____

_____

What do you remember most about your wedding day?

_____

_____

_____

What are your best memories from the first year of marriage?

_____

_____

_____

What are your best memories from the past twelve months?

_____

_____

_____

PART 2: WHAT'S GREAT ABOUT US!

1. The three things I'd say are most positive about our relationship right now are:
    1. _____
    2. _____
    3. _____

2. Two things that are fine about our relationship but could be better are:
    1. _____
    2. _____

3. One thing I could do to make our relationship better is:
    1. _____

POST-DATE APPLICATION

- Look for the positives. Find ways to compliment each other between now and the next date.

- Do that one thing you know you can do to make your marriage better.

- Read chapter 2, "Learning to Communicate," and complete the Date Two Exercise.

Learning to
COMMUNICATE

This date will help you connect and talk together on a deeper level as you share your feelings and learn to really listen in a way that brings you closer together.

PREPARATION

- Read chapter 2, "Learning to Communicate."

- Complete Date Two Exercise.

- Choose a location for your date that will allow you to talk quietly—perhaps a picnic in a park or a quiet coffee shop.

DATE NIGHT TIPS

- Talk through the exercise one question at a time.

- Be prepared for some surprises and new insights about your spouse. This new knowledge can add depth to your relationship.

- Stay positive. If conflicts arise in the course of your conversation, note and table them to discuss later. Devote your conversation solely to the focus of the date.

CHAPTER SUMMARY

How open are your lines of communication? Do you say what you mean and mean what you say? How well do you really listen? When your partner is talking, are you listening or strategizing your response? The purpose of communication in marriage is to be heard and understood. A large part of communication is nonverbal (55 percent) and tone of voice (38 percent). That only leaves 7 percent for the words! But words are so important. By understanding three communication styles, you can learn how to share your deeper emotions in a way that does not attack the other person or make your partner feel defensive.

You can use a simple communication formula for sharing your feelings in an appropriate way. For example, start your sentence with "I" and express your feelings—"I feel frustrated when it's time for dinner and you're not home yet and haven't called to say you're running late." Then say, "Now, tell me how you feel," and really listen. Date Two will help you listen on a deeper level so you'll be able to talk together in ways that build better communication.

Learning to Communicate

TALKING TOPICS

1. What are your favorite topics to talk about? For example, things about which you usually agree, look forward to discussing, and that promote positive interaction between you.

2. What are your least favorite topics to talk about? For example, things you tend to avoid, debate, or that promote negative interaction between you. (Just list them here. Don't talk about them. Save them for the next date.)

SHARING OUR FEELINGS

Take turns completing the following sentence starters.

- When you give me a compliment, I feel...

- When you express appreciation for something I did, I feel...

- When you smile at me, I feel...

- When you make a sacrifice for me, I feel...

- When you reach out and touch me, I feel...

- When you tell me you love me, I feel...

- When you tell me you are proud of me, I feel...

POST-DATE APPLICATION

- Keep looking for ways to compliment each other between now and the next date.

- Try to identify the triggers that get you into the confronting style of communication so you can stop before things escalate.

- Practice using your red flag cues such as, "Ouch, I feel a pinch."

- Try to make intentional use of the connecting style at least once a day.

- Read chapter 3, "Solving Problems as a Couple," and complete the Date Three Exercise.

Learning to Communicate

TALKING TOPICS

1. What are your favorite topics to talk about? For example, things about which you usually agree, look forward to discussing, and that promote positive interaction between you.

2. What are your least favorite topics to talk about? For example, things you tend to avoid, debate, or that promote negative interaction between you. (Just list them here. Don't talk about them. Save them for the next date.)

SHARING OUR FEELINGS

Take turns completing the following sentence starters.

- When you give me a compliment, I feel...

- When you express appreciation for something I did, I feel...

- When you smile at me, I feel...

- When you make a sacrifice for me, I feel...

- When you reach out and touch me, I feel...

- When you tell me you love me, I feel...

- When you tell me you are proud of me, I feel...

POST-DATE APPLICATION

- Keep looking for ways to compliment each other between now and the next date.

- Try to identify the triggers that get you into the confronting style of communication so you can stop before things escalate.

- Practice using your red flag cues such as, "Ouch, I feel a pinch."

- Try to make intentional use of the connecting style at least once a day.

- Read chapter 3, "Solving Problems as a Couple," and complete the Date Three Exercise.

Solving Problems as a
COUPLE

This date will help you learn ways to talk about issues and manage and solve problems as a couple that will build your relationship instead of tearing it down.

PREPARATION

- Read chapter 3, "Solving Problems as a Couple."

- Complete Part 1 of the Date Three Exercise. Read through Parts 2–5.

- Choose a location that will allow you to talk quietly — perhaps a park bench or quiet coffee shop. Even your local zoo might be fun for this date.

DATE NIGHT TIPS

- Review the communication tips in "Smart Tips for Great Dates" (page 160).

- Continue to look for new insights about your spouse. This exercise can open new opportunities for growth and intimacy in your relationship.

- If conflicts arise that are too uncomfortable, write them down and save for later. Don't try to deal with them on this date!

CHAPTER SUMMARY

If you take two imperfect people and expect them to live together harmoniously and problem free, you're in for a surprise. Every couple experiences problems from time to time and 69 percent of the issues we disagree about are of the perpetual variety—they are not going to be solved or go away. Instead, we need to learn how to manage them. We also need to be able handle and process anger. How do you handle your anger? How would you *like* to handle your anger? Making an anger contract will help you process your anger. By using the feelings formula (from chapter 2) and the speaker/listener technique, you can express your negative emotions in a way that is not attacking.

Once you fully understand how you both feel about an issue, together you can go through the steps to resolve or manage this issue. If you reach a stalemate, the most positive thing you can do is to get help. In most instances, if you are willing to pull together, to attack the problem and not each other, to process anger and work together, you will find a way to manage or solve the problem. Remember to start with an issue that is not too emotional or volatile! After some initial successes, you can go on to weightier issues. Top off this date by doing something fun to celebrate that you're learning how to manage problems as a couple.

Solving Problems as a Couple

PART 1: YOU AND YOUR FRIENDS AT THE ZOO

Before your date, rate yourself. Then on your date compare your lists and rankings. Then remember, you don't have to live at the zoo.

Which animal character do you identify with the most in handling conflict?

_____ Turtle (I withdraw) _____ Chameleon (I yield)

_____ Skunk (I attack) _____ Owl (I intellectualize)

_____ Beaver (I avoid) _____ Gorilla (I intimidate)

How does the animal you relate to bring out the animal in your spouse? How could you respond differently in times of conflict?

PART 2: MAKE AN ANGER CONTRACT

- We will tell each other when we are getting angry.

- We will not vent our anger at each other.

- We will ask for the other's help in solving whatever problem is causing the anger.

Signed: _____ Signed: _____

PART 3: IDENTIFY THE PROBLEM

From Date Two Exercise, under "least favorite topics," together choose the least emotional topic and write it here. Then talk about it using the speaker/listener technique.

You can review the rules for using the speaker/listener technique on page 49. Remember, you're not trying to solve the issue but to understand each other's perspective.

NOTE: If you find yourself falling into a negative pattern, skip directly to Part 5, then return to this exercise at a later time. Now you're ready to talk about solutions.

PART 4: SOLVE THE PROBLEM

Step One: Define the problem. (You just did this using the speaker/listener technique. Write it down here.) _____

_____

Step Two: Identify who has the need.

Step Three: Brainstorm solutions.

Step Four: Identify a plan of action.

PART 5: TREAT YOURSELF!

Enough work for one date! Stop at your favorite frozen yogurt or ice cream shop on your way home. Celebrate the progress you have made in being able to talk about touchy subjects. And if you discovered some really touchy subjects, don't touch them. Save them for another time.

POST-DATE APPLICATION

- When you feel yourself getting angry, follow the steps in the anger contract you just signed.

- Continue to practice using the speaker/listener technique and the feelings formula to work through disagreements.

- If you didn't complete Part 4 on your date, find a time to do so this week.

- Read chapter 4, "Becoming an Encourager," and complete the Date Four Exercise.

Solving Problems as a Couple

PART 1: YOU AND YOUR FRIENDS AT THE ZOO

Before your date, rate yourself. Then on your date compare your lists and rankings. Then remember, you don't have to live at the zoo.

Which animal character do you identify with the most in handling conflict?

_____ Turtle (I withdraw) _____ Chameleon (I yield)

_____ Skunk (I attack)   _____ Owl (I intellectualize)

_____ Beaver (I avoid)   _____ Gorilla (I intimidate)

How does the animal you relate to bring out the animal in your spouse? How could you respond differently in times of conflict?

PART 2: MAKE AN ANGER CONTRACT

- We will tell each other when we are getting angry.

- We will not vent our anger at each other.

- We will ask for the other's help in solving whatever problem is causing the anger.

Signed: _____ Signed: _____

PART 3: IDENTIFY THE PROBLEM

From Date Two Exercise, under "least favorite topics," together choose the least emotional topic and write it here. Then talk about it using the speaker/listener technique.

You can review the rules for using the speaker/listener technique on page 49. Remember, you're not trying to solve the issue but to understand each other's perspective.

NOTE: If you find yourself falling into a negative pattern, skip directly to Part 5, then return to this exercise at a later time. Now you're ready to talk about solutions.

PART 4: SOLVE THE PROBLEM

Step One: Define the problem. (You just did this using the speaker/listener technique. Write it down here.) _____

_____

Step Two: Identify who has the need.

Step Three: Brainstorm solutions.

Step Four: Identify a plan of action.

PART 5: TREAT YOURSELF!

Enough work for one date! Stop at your favorite frozen yogurt or ice cream shop on your way home. Celebrate the progress you have made in being able to talk about touchy subjects. And if you discovered some really touchy subjects, don't touch them. Save them for another time.

POST-DATE APPLICATION

- When you feel yourself getting angry, follow the steps in the anger contract you just signed.

- Continue to practice using the speaker/listener technique and the feelings formula to work through disagreements.

- If you didn't complete Part 4 on your date, find a time to do so this week.

- Read chapter 4, "Becoming an Encourager," and complete the Date Four Exercise.

Becoming an ENCOURAGER

On this date you will look at ways to encourage each other and ways to increase the fun factor in your relationship.

PREPARATION

- Read chapter 4, "Becoming an Encourager."

- Complete the Date Four Exercise.

- Bring a small notebook or journal, two notecards, and two envelopes on your date.

- Consider combining this date with an activity you like to do together such as hiking, fishing, golfing, tennis, or playing board games.

DATE NIGHT TIPS

- One at a time, talk about your responses to each of the questions from the exercise.

- Keep the emphasis on fun.

- Leave all problems and issues at home.

CHAPTER SUMMARY

Before marriage, it's easy to look for the positive. But once we marry, the stars in our eyes begin to fade and we see each other's little idiosyncrasies. The reality of living together creates tension, and without realizing what is happening we can easily focus on the negative instead of the positive. Psychologists tell us it takes at least five positive statements to offset one negative statement, so we need to develop the habit of building each other up by focusing on the positive. Date Four will guide you in how to give honest praise by sincerely describing what you appreciate about your spouse. Laughter is a first cousin of encouragement. Look for ways to laugh together. Laughter relieves tension, lowers your stress level, and is good for the health of your marriage.

Becoming an Encourager

Use the following to help you focus on areas in which you can begin to encourage your spouse and ways in which you hope your spouse might encourage you.

PART ONE: ENCOURAGING QUESTIONS

1. How has your spouse encouraged you in the past?

2. How would you like your spouse to encourage you in the future?

3. What are five things you appreciate about your spouse? Think of thoughtful actions and/or qualities you appreciate, such as...

PART TWO: ENCOURAGING ACTIVITIES

Choose one or more of these activities.

1. Use your list in the last question above to start a positive journal. The idea is to have a notebook/journal that you can leave around your home where you both will see it often — like in the bathroom. Take turns making positive entries. Initiate your journal on this date.

2. Use the two blank notecards and envelopes that you brought on your date to write a note of appreciation to your spouse. Seal it. Hide it at home where your spouse will find it this week.

3. Make a coupon book of fun dates you want to have with each other in the future. (You can do an online search for "coupon books for couples" to get some good ideas.) Is there an area that you would like to explore together? (Sports, crafts, writing, gourmet cooking, hobbies, education, etc.)

4. On your date stop by the dollar store and pick out a small but thoughtful gift for each other.

POST-DATE APPLICATION

- For one day this week, keep track of the number of positive and negative statements you make to your spouse. Repeat the practice each day until you reach a ratio of at least five positives for every one negative statement.

- Write entries this week in your positive journal.

- Be appreciative when your spouse compliments you.

- Look for humor and reasons to laugh together!

- Read chapter 5, "Finding Unity in Diversity," and complete the Date Five Exercise.

Becoming an Encourager

Use the following to help you focus on areas in which you can begin to encourage your spouse and ways in which you hope your spouse might encourage you.

PART ONE: ENCOURAGING QUESTIONS

1. How has your spouse encouraged you in the past?

2. How would you like your spouse to encourage you in the future?

3. What are five things you appreciate about your spouse? Think of thoughtful actions and/or qualities you appreciate, such as...

PART TWO: ENCOURAGING ACTIVITIES

Choose one or more of these activities.

1. Use your list in the last question above to start a positive journal. The idea is to have a notebook/journal that you can leave around your home where you both will see it often—like in the bathroom. Take turns making positive entries. Initiate your journal on this date.

2. Use the two blank notecards and envelopes that you brought on your date to write a note of appreciation to your spouse. Seal it. Hide it at home where your spouse will find it this week.

3. Make a coupon book of fun dates you want to have with each other in the future. (You can do an online search for "coupon books for couples" to get some good ideas.) Is there an area that you would like to explore together? (Sports, crafts, writing, gourmet cooking, hobbies, education, etc.)

4. On your date stop by the dollar store and pick out a small but thoughtful gift for each other.

POST-DATE APPLICATION

- For one day this week, keep track of the number of positive and negative statements you make to your spouse. Repeat the practice each day until you reach a ratio of at least five positives for every one negative statement.

- Write entries this week in your positive journal.

- Be appreciative when your spouse compliments you.

- Look for humor and reasons to laugh together!

- Read chapter 5, "Finding Unity in Diversity," and complete the Date Five Exercise.

Finding Unity in

DIVERSITY

This date gives you the opportunity to focus on how you can benefit from each other's strengths and complement each other in the ways you're different.

PREPARATION

- Read chapter 5, "Finding Unity in Diversity."

- Complete the Date Five Exercise.

- Plan to spend your date at your favorite hangout, — ideally a place where you can talk privately.

DATE NIGHT TIPS

- While discussing your dating exercise, concentrate on each other's strengths.

- You might want to make a list of your couple strengths. This will help you appreciate how you balance each other's weaknesses.

CHAPTER SUMMARY

In creating a marriage that honors unity and diversity, the challenge is to understand and appreciate the unique strengths evident in your similarities and differences. Your weak areas may be your spouse's strong areas. Instead of being threatened by your partner's strengths, we encourage you to celebrate them.

On this date you will have the opportunity to talk about the ways you are different and the ways you are alike. Taking time to assess your unique attributes will help you to build a strong marriage team by appreciating each other's differences. As teammates, you can balance each other out and work together to form a strong partnership.

DATE FIVE EXERCISE

Finding Unity in Diversity

PART 1: IDENTIFY YOURSELF

Use the seven continuums below to assess your tendencies. Mark an
X on each continuum to indicate your own tendencies. Then mark
an **O** to indicate how you assess your spouse's tendencies.

PRIVATE	PUBLIC

SPONTANEOUS	PLANNER

LIVE WIRE	LAID-BACK

EARLY BIRD	NIGHT OWL

FEELINGS-ORIENTED	FACTS-ORIENTED

TIME-FOCUSED	NOT TIME-FOCUSED

SAVER	SPENDER

PART 2: TALK ABOUT YOUR TEAM

1. Discuss what the continuums reveal about the ways you are different. What, if anything, surprises you?

2. Now discuss what the continuums reveal about the ways you are alike. Again, any surprises?

3. In what ways would you say your differences balance each other and are or could be couple strengths?

4. In what areas are you so similar that your tendencies might pose a liability? How might you compensate?

5. How does the concept of viewing your marriage as "a team" impact your relationship? Make a list of your combined strengths—the strengths of your marriage team.

POST-DATE APPLICATION

- Keep looking for ways your differences complement and strengthen your relationship.

- In ways that you are alike, keep looking for ways you can compensate!

- Read chapter 6, "Building a Creative Love Life," and complete the Date Six Exercise.

Finding Unity in Diversity

PART 1: IDENTIFY YOURSELF

Use the seven continuums below to assess your tendencies. Mark an X on each continuum to indicate your own tendencies. Then mark an O to indicate how you assess your spouse's tendencies.

PRIVATE	PUBLIC

SPONTANEOUS	PLANNER

LIVE WIRE	LAID-BACK

EARLY BIRD	NIGHT OWL

FEELINGS-ORIENTED	FACTS-ORIENTED

TIME-FOCUSED	NOT TIME-FOCUSED

SAVER	SPENDER

PART 2: TALK ABOUT YOUR TEAM

1. Discuss what the continuums reveal about the ways you are different. What, if anything, surprises you?

2. Now discuss what the continuums reveal about the ways you are alike. Again, any surprises?

3. In what ways would you say your differences balance each other and are or could be couple strengths?

4. In what areas are you so similar that your tendencies might pose a liability? How might you compensate?

5. How does the concept of viewing your marriage as "a team" impact your relationship? Make a list of your combined strengths—the strengths of your marriage team.

POST-DATE APPLICATION

- Keep looking for ways your differences complement and strengthen your relationship.

- In ways that you are alike, keep looking for ways you can compensate!

- Read chapter 6, "Building a Creative Love Life," and complete the Date Six Exercise.

Building a Creative
LOVE LIFE

This date will help you define what intimacy, love, and romance means to you. You'll talk about ways to energize your love life and get your desires and expectations in sync.

PREPARATION

- Read chapter 6, "Building a Creative Love Life."

- Complete the Date Six Exercise.

- If you can plan ahead and get away overnight for this date, bravo! Otherwise, choose a romantic restaurant or café where you can talk privately.

DATE NIGHT TIPS

- While this date is by far the most popular date, discussing this topic is tough for some people. Be sensitive to the other. Open up to your partner and share your feelings. (You might want to review chapter 2.)

- Be inventive and thoughtful about ways to make this date romantic—holding hands, going for a stroll in the moonlight, or taking a walk in the rain.

CHAPTER SUMMARY

If you want to have a creative love life, stop having sex and start making love. When the newlywed hormones settle down—and they will—it's easy for your sex life to end up on the back burner. Life happens. Romance and intimacy fade. Boredom creeps in. Couples need to guard against "adventure lust." Affairs usually don't happen overnight, but spouses who are tired, isolated, and romantically starved are vulnerable. Invest in the following components for a creative romantic love life:

- *Trust: Feeling safe with each other*

- *Mutuality: Freely choosing to love each other*

- *Honesty: Openly communicating your true feelings*

- *Intimacy: Knowing and being known*

- *Sensuality: Giving and receiving pleasure*

- *Sex: Joining together physically*

Having a creative love life is not an optional add-on; it's a vital part of growing and solidifying your marriage. Be proactive in building a creative love life. Loving for a lifetime may just make your "lifetime" longer and more enjoyable. Research says you will live longer, look ten years younger, and have even better sex after fifty years of marriage.

Building a Creative Love Life

PART 1: WHAT IS MOST IMPORTANT TO YOU?

Listed below are six components of a romantic love life. On a scale of 1 to 5 (1 being *not important* and 5 being *very important*), rank how important each component is to you.

_____ Trust: Feeling safe with each other

_____ Mutuality: Freely choosing to love each other

_____ Honesty: Openly communicating your true feelings

_____ Intimacy: Knowing and being known

_____ Sensuality: Giving and receiving pleasure

_____ Sex: Joining together physically

PART 1: TAKING THE SAT (SEXUAL ATTITUDE TEST)

Rate the following statements on a scale from 1 to 5 (1 being *strongly disagree* and 5 being *strongly agree*).

_____ I enjoy my sexual relationship with my spouse.

_____ I think my spouse enjoys our sexual relationship.

_____ I look forward to the next time of physical intimacy.

_____ I am satisfied with our sex life.

_____ My spouse tells me he/she is satisfied with our sex life.

_____ I initiate lovemaking from time to time.

_____ I plan times for us to be alone together.

_____ We have had an overnight getaway (alone) in the past six months.

_____ I often tell my spouse that I desire him/her.

_____ My spouse would describe me as a tender lover.

_____ I'm willing to work on areas in our sexual relationship that need improvement.

Now share your responses from both lists and discuss your similarities and differences. This exercise will help you honestly communicate your true feelings with each other and initiate a positive communication going forward.

PART 3: PLAN A GETAWAY (OPTIONAL)

Use the following questions to discuss and plan your ultimate getaway.

1. Where would we like to go? Make a list of possible places, then choose one.

2. When can we go? Choose possible dates and add the getaway to your calendar.

3. What are our resources for our getaway? Work out a budget and designate funds.

4. What arrangements do we need to make? (Childcare, pet care, reservations, etc.)

5. Talk about your expectations for your getaway. Do you want to go to Alabama, Florida, or Georgia? (See our story on page 92.)

POST-DATE APPLICATION

- Look for ways to be more sensual with each other this week.

- Look back over the chapter and choose one thing you could to do this week to add a little romance to your marriage.

- Follow up on your plans for a getaway. Even twenty-four hours can make a big difference.

- Read chapter 7, "Sharing Responsibility and Working Together," and complete the Date Seven Exercise.

DATE SIX EXERCISE

Building a Creative Love Life

PART 1: WHAT IS MOST IMPORTANT TO YOU?

Listed below are six components of a romantic love life. On a scale of 1 to 5 (1 being *not important* and 5 being *very important*), rank how important each component is to you.

_____ Trust: Feeling safe with each other

_____ Mutuality: Freely choosing to love each other

_____ Honesty: Openly communicating your true feelings

_____ Intimacy: Knowing and being known

_____ Sensuality: Giving and receiving pleasure

_____ Sex: Joining together physically

PART 1: TAKING THE SAT (SEXUAL ATTITUDE TEST)

Rate the following statements on a scale from 1 to 5 (1 being *strongly disagree* and 5 being *strongly agree*).

_____ I enjoy my sexual relationship with my spouse.

_____ I think my spouse enjoys our sexual relationship.

_____ I look forward to the next time of physical intimacy.

_____ I am satisfied with our sex life.

_____ My spouse tells me he/she is satisfied with our sex life.

_____ I initiate lovemaking from time to time.

_____ I plan times for us to be alone together.

_____ We have had an overnight getaway (alone) in the past six months.

_____ I often tell my spouse that I desire him/her.

_____ My spouse would describe me as a tender lover.

_____ I'm willing to work on areas in our sexual relationship that need improvement.

Now share your responses from both lists and discuss your similarities and differences. This exercise will help you honestly communicate your true feelings with each other and initiate a positive communication going forward.

PART 3: PLAN A GETAWAY (OPTIONAL)

Use the following questions to discuss and plan your ultimate getaway.

1. Where would we like to go? Make a list of possible places, then choose one.

2. When can we go? Choose possible dates and add the getaway to your calendar.

3. What are our resources for our getaway? Work out a budget and designate funds.

4. What arrangements do we need to make? (Childcare, pet care, reservations, etc.)

5. Talk about your expectations for your getaway. Do you want to go to Alabama, Florida, or Georgia? (See our story on page 90.)

POST-DATE APPLICATION

- Look for ways to be more sensual with each other this week.

- Look back over the chapter and choose one thing you could to do this week to add a little romance to your marriage.

- Follow up on your plans for a getaway. Even twenty-four hours can make a big difference.

- Read chapter 7, "Sharing Responsibility and Working Together," and complete the Date Seven Exercise.

Sharing Responsibility and
WORKING TOGETHER

This date will help you talk about how you want to divide and/ or share chores and life tasks including setting financial goals and making lifestyle choices.

PREPARATION

- Read chapter 7, "Sharing Responsibility and Working Together."

- Complete the Date Seven Exercise.

- Choose a location where you can talk. You might want to go out for dinner so neither of you will have to cook, clean the kitchen, or wash the dishes.

DATE NIGHT TIPS

- This date doesn't have to be work! Concentrate on finding balance.

- Attack the responsibilities, not each other.

- Use creative brainstorming to find helpful solutions.

- Reward yourself by ordering dessert.

CHAPTER SUMMARY

Did you know that research reveals that spouses who more equally share home responsibilities have better sex? When husband and wife share the workload, both get much-needed help, resulting in more time and more desire to make love. So maybe there is something really sexy when your partner pushes the vacuum or does the dishes. Seriously, divvying up household chores can be a real issue for couples—especially for those who are trying to balance jobs outside the home—but when we tackle responsibilities and work together as a team, we both benefit.

On this date you will get to look at your present responsibilities and make adjustments as needed that will bring more balance into your lives. Defining and evaluating your financial goals is also helpful. Are you working harder and enjoying life less? By evaluating how you invest time and money and choosing your lifestyle carefully, you may discover that less is more. You may also discover that it's fun to team up. Working together and sharing responsibilities can be one of your most rewarding jobs!

Sharing Responsibility and Working Together

PART 1: ASSESSING AND BALANCING YOUR RESPONSIBILITIES

1. Assess your present responsibilities.

List your responsibilities outside the home:

Husband   **Wife**

_____   _____
_____   _____
_____   _____
_____   _____
_____   _____
_____   _____

List your responsibilities inside the home:

Husband   **Wife**

_____   _____
_____   _____
_____   _____
_____   _____
_____   _____
_____   _____

2. Consider how you might need to rebalance home responsibilities.

From the home responsibilities listed above, combine all the household jobs and responsibilities, such as preparing meals, cleaning the house, doing the laundry, helping the children with homework, and caring for the yard.

From the combined list, choose the jobs you do or prefer to do (you may choose basically the same tasks you are presenting doing, but it's also a chance to find more balance in who does what in the home):

Husband	Wife
_____	_____
_____	_____
_____	_____
_____	_____
_____	_____

Brainstorm solutions for how to address the tasks that are on neither of your lists—the tasks neither of you wants to do. Maybe you can get help from your kids with household chores or perhaps hire someone to help (such as a cleaning service to come once a month or a neighborhood teen to mow the lawn).

Briefly summarize your decisions and your new plan below.

_____

_____

_____

PART 2: MANAGING YOUR MONEY TOGETHER

1. What short- and long-term financial goals would you like to set for the future? (If you already have financial goals, use this date to have a checkup and assess how you're doing in reaching your goals.)
2. Talk about which of our tips would be helpful to you in managing your money?
   - Track what you spend for the next month.
   - Limit credit card spending to what you can pay off each month.
   - Use cash for everyday expenses.
   - Start saving each month; even a small amount can make a different to your future.
   - Experience the joy of giving.
3. Talk about lifestyle choices (where you live, what you spend money for such as cars, clothes and so on) as it relates to achieving your financial goals.

POST-DATE APPLICATION

- Monitor your new plans for working together.
- Have the mindset that you are going to work together.
- Choose one of the financial tips to apply and try this week.
- Read chapter 8, "Balancing Your Roles as Partner and Parent," and complete the Date Eight Exercise.

Sharing Responsibility and Working Together

PART 1: ASSESSING AND BALANCING YOUR RESPONSIBILITIES

1. Assess your present responsibilities.

List your responsibilities outside the home:

Husband   **Wife**

_____   _____
_____   _____
_____   _____
_____   _____
_____   _____

List your responsibilities inside the home:

Husband   **Wife**

_____   _____
_____   _____
_____   _____
_____   _____
_____   _____

2. Consider how you might need to rebalance home responsibilities.

From the home responsibilities listed above, combine all the household jobs and responsibilities, such as preparing meals, cleaning the house, doing the laundry, helping the children with homework, and caring for the yard.

From the combined list, choose the jobs you do or prefer to do (you may choose basically the same tasks you are presenting doing, but it's also a chance to find more balance in who does what in the home):

Husband	**Wife**
_____	_____
_____	_____
_____	_____
_____	_____

Brainstorm solutions for how to address the tasks that are on neither of your lists—the tasks neither of you wants to do. Maybe you can get help from your kids with household chores or perhaps hire someone to help (such as a cleaning service to come once a month or a neighborhood teen to mow the lawn).

Briefly summarize your decisions and your new plan below.

_____

_____

_____

PART 2: MANAGING YOUR MONEY TOGETHER

1. What short- and long-term financial goals would you like to set for the future? (If you already have financial goals, use this date to have a checkup and assess how you're doing in reaching your goals.)

2. Talk about which of our tips would be helpful to you in managing your money?
   - Track what you spend for the next month.
   - Limit credit card spending to what you can pay off each month.
   - Use cash for everyday expenses.
   - Start saving each month; even a small amount can make a different to your future.
   - Experience the joy of giving.

3. Talk about lifestyle choices (where you live, what you spend money for such as cars, clothes and so on) as it relates to achieving your financial goals.

POST-DATE APPLICATION

   - Monitor your new plans for working together.
   - Have the mindset that you are going to work together.
   - Choose one of the financial tips to apply and try this week.
   - Read chapter 8, "Balancing Your Roles as Partner and Parent," and complete the Date Eight Exercise.

Balancing Your Roles as
PARTNER AND PARENT

This date will help you better understand how your children influence your marriage and how your marriage influences your children. Both can be positive!

PREPARATION

- Read chapter 8, "Balancing Your Roles as Partner and Parent."
- Complete the Date Eight Exercise.

DATE NIGHT TIPS

- Keep the focus of your conversation on how your children affect your relationship.
- This is not a time to try to solve your children's problems or to talk about homework issue or curfews.

CHAPTER SUMMARY

NOTE: We understand that this topic can be a very sensitive area for some couples who are not parents. If you feel it would be best to skip over this date, we give you permission to do so. Go out on your date and do something for fun!

Enriching your marriage while parenting your children is not an oxymoron, even though it seems like one. Your role as a partner does not have to compete with your role as a parent. However, balancing your roles can be challenging. It may help to realize the ways children can enrich your marriage. For instance, they are a continual reminder that you are one; they foster teamwork and creativity as you work to find time together; and they check the honesty and transparency of your own communication. At the same time, when you take seriously the challenge to build a strong and healthy marriage, you will enrich your children's lives and their future marriage. You are their model for how to build healthy relationships. You teach them life skills and pass on traditions and values. Remember, little eyes are watching you. Whatever your family situation (if you are a grandparent, aunt, uncle, and so on) you are a model to those around you.

Balancing Your Roles as Partner and Parent

PART 1: HOW OUR CHILDREN ENRICH OUR MARRIAGE

Use the following prompts to reflect on how your children enrich your marriage.

1. Our children remind us that we're one when . . .

2. Our children foster teamwork in us when . . .

3. Our children help us to appreciate one another when . . .

4. Our children promote creativity in our lives when . . .

5. Our children check our communication and keep us honest when . . .

6. Our children prevent boredom when . . .

7. Some of the rewards we've experienced in marriage because of our children are . . .

8. Optional: Our grandchildren have enriched our marriage by . . .

PART 2: HOW OUR MARRIAGE ENRICHES OUR CHILDREN

Use the following prompts to reflect on how your marriage enriches your children.

1. We provide security, love, and a sense of belonging when . . .

2. We model healthy relationships when . . .

3. We give guidance and leadership when . . .

4. We teach life skills when . . .

5. We pass on traditions and values when . . .

PART 3: FAMILY PLANNING (FOR COUPLES CONSIDERING STARTING A FAMILY)

If you don't yet have children but plan to, use the following questions to reflect on your hopes and expectations for parenthood. On your date, share your responses with one another.

1. How many children would you like to have?

2. What would be the ideal spacing of children (e.g., two years apart)?

3. What are your favorite names? How would you feel about using traditional family names for your child?

4. How do you feel about childcare?

5. How would you still find time for the two of you with a new baby in the house?

6. What is your concept of "co-parenting" (i.e., how much time and energy you both invest in parenting your children)?

7. If you can't have biological children, would you want to consider other options such as adoption or foster care?

POST-DATE APPLICATION

- Look for the positive ways your children impact your marriage.

- Look for the positive ways your marriage impacts your children.

- Read chapter 9, "Connecting Faith, Love, and Marriage," and complete the Date Nine Exercise.

Balancing Your Roles as Partner and Parent

PART 1: HOW OUR CHILDREN ENRICH OUR MARRIAGE

Use the following prompts to reflect on how your children enrich your marriage.

1. Our children remind us that we're one when ...

2. Our children foster teamwork in us when ...

3. Our children help us to appreciate one another when ...

4. Our children promote creativity in our lives when ...

5. Our children check our communication and keep us honest when ...

6. Our children prevent boredom when ...

7. Some of the rewards we've experienced in marriage because of our children are ...

8. Optional: Our grandchildren have enriched our marriage by ...

PART 2: HOW OUR MARRIAGE ENRICHES OUR CHILDREN

Use the following prompts to reflect on how your marriage enriches your children.

1. We provide security, love, and a sense of belonging when ...

2. We model healthy relationships when ...

3. We give guidance and leadership when ...

4. We teach life skills when ...

5. We pass on traditions and values when ...

PART 3: FAMILY PLANNING (FOR COUPLES CONSIDERING STARTING A FAMILY)

If you don't yet have children but plan to, use the following questions to reflect on your hopes and expectations for parenthood. On your date, share your responses with one another.

1. How many children would you like to have?

2. What would be the ideal spacing of children (e.g., two years apart)?

3. What are your favorite names? How would you feel about using traditional family names for your child?

4. How do you feel about childcare?

5. How would you still find time for the two of you with a new baby in the house?

6. What is your concept of "co-parenting" (i.e., how much time and energy you both invest in parenting your children)?

7. If you can't have biological children, would you want to consider other options such as adoption or foster care?

POST-DATE APPLICATION

- Look for the positive ways your children impact your marriage.

- Look for the positive ways your marriage impacts your children.

- Read chapter 9, "Connecting Faith, Love, and Marriage," and complete the Date Nine Exercise.

Connecting Faith, Love, and
MARRIAGE

On this date you will have the opportunity to share your spiritual journeys and talk about your core values and how you can connect your faith and love.

PREPARATION

- Read chapter 9, "Connecting Faith, Love, and Marriage."

- Complete the Date Nine Exercise.

- Choose a location where you can quietly reflect together.

DATE NIGHT TIPS

- If you are at different places on your spiritual journey, be sensitive to one another.

- Focus on what you have in common rather than your differences.

- This is an opportunity to share your inner feelings. It is not a time to try to change your spouse.

CHAPTER SUMMARY

Sharing core beliefs and living out these beliefs in your marriage can help you connect faith and love in your marriage. It is important to first understand your own belief system, which includes your values, ethics, and core beliefs, and then find the common bonds between you. These commonalities form the foundation for your shared belief system and are the springboard for developing a spiritual dimension to your relationship. Your faith connection can then manifest itself in unconditional love and acceptance, forgiveness, prayer, and service to one another as well as others.

Connecting Faith, Love, and Marriage

Connecting faith, love, and marriage involves building spiritual intimacy with each other and with God. On this date you'll talk about factors that can bring you closer together spiritually.

PART 1 – TAKING A COUPLE SPIRITUAL EXPERIENCE SURVEY

On a scale of 1 to 5 (5 being very effective and 1 being not so effective), rate how each facet helps you connect spiritually with your partner. Now rate them as you think your partner would rate them. Compare your list and discuss.

W   H

_____ _____ Serving others together

_____ _____ Experiencing nature together

_____ _____ Having devotions together

_____ _____ Praying together

_____ _____ Attending religious services together

_____ _____ Getting together with other couples

_____ _____ Giving to others

_____ _____ Celebrating religious holidays

PART 2 – CONSIDER FOUR CORE BELIEFS/ VALUES FROM CHAPTER 9

How do these core beliefs help you to connect your faith and love?

1. Unconditional Love and Acceptance

Check the traits that describe you.

☐ Patient   ☐ Kind   ☐ Grace-filled

☐ Trustworthy   ☐ Forgiving   ☐ Persevering

2. Forgiveness

How easy is it for you to forgive your spouse and ask for forgiveness when needed?

Is there anything you need to ask forgiveness for right now?

3. Prayer

Praying together gives couples a unique spiritual connection. From the list below check the ones that would be most comfortable to you to try.

_____ Share a list of prayer requests with each other.

_____ Pray silently together.

_____ Agree to pray for one another — separately.

_____ Each of you pray out loud.

_____ Keep a prayer journal together.

_____ Pray together as you walk or hike.

4. Service

Make a list of service projects that you could do together and choose one (helping at a soup kitchen, inner-city mission, volunteering to help a single parent, and so on).

POST-DATE APPLICATION

- Choose a book on this a topic and commit to reading it together in the coming month.

- For ten more Great Dates on this topic, see our book *10 Great Dates: Connecting Faith, Love and Marriage.*

- Read chapter 10, "Achieving an Intentional Marriage," and complete the Date Ten Exercise.

Connecting Faith, Love, and Marriage

Connecting faith, love, and marriage involves building spiritual intimacy with each other and with God. On this date you'll talk about factors that can bring you closer together spiritually.

PART 1 – TAKING A COUPLE SPIRITUAL EXPERIENCE SURVEY

On a scale of 1 to 5 (5 being very effective and 1 being not so effective), rate how each facet helps you connect spiritually with your partner. Now rate them as you think your partner would rate them. Compare your list and discuss.

W   H

_____ _____ Serving others together
_____ _____ Experiencing nature together
_____ _____ Having devotions together
_____ _____ Praying together
_____ _____ Attending religious services together
_____ _____ Getting together with other couples
_____ _____ Giving to others
_____ _____ Celebrating religious holidays

PART 2 – CONSIDER FOUR CORE BELIEFS/ VALUES FROM CHAPTER 9

How do these core beliefs help you to connect your faith and love?

1. Unconditional Love and Acceptance
Check the traits that describe you.

☐ Patient   ☐ Kind   ☐ Grace-filled
☐ Trustworthy   ☐ Forgiving   ☐ Persevering

2. Forgiveness

How easy is it for you to forgive your spouse and ask for forgiveness when needed?

Is there anything you need to ask forgiveness for right now?

3. Prayer

Praying together gives couples a unique spiritual connection. From the list below check the ones that would be most comfortable to you to try.

_____ Share a list of prayer requests with each other.

_____ Pray silently together.

_____ Agree to pray for one another—separately.

_____ Each of you pray out loud.

_____ Keep a prayer journal together.

_____ Pray together as you walk or hike.

4. Service

Make a list of service projects that you could do together and choose one (helping at a soup kitchen, inner-city mission, volunteering to help a single parent, and so on).

POST-DATE APPLICATION

- Choose a book on this a topic and commit to reading it together in the coming month.

- For ten more Great Dates on this topic, see our book *10 Great Dates: Connecting Faith, Love and Marriage*.

- Read chapter 10, "Achieving an Intentional Marriage," and complete the Date Ten Exercise.

Achieving an Intentional
MARRIAGE

This date will encourage you to set practical goals to help you turn your desires and dreams for your marriage into reality.

PREPARATION

- Read chapter 10, "Achieving an Intentional Marriage."

- Complete Part 1 of the Date Ten Exercise. Review Parts 2 and 3.

- Choose a location where you can have access to a table. Your local library might be a fun place for this date.

DATE NIGHT TIPS

- Take your time; don't race through this date.

- Set at least one goal that you both want to achieve, but don't be overambitious. It's better to set one goal you can reach than to have ten you can't reach.

CHAPTER SUMMARY

You can have an intentional marriage by talking about your expectations, evaluating your present degree of marriage involvement, setting goals, and monitoring your progress. If you and your spouse were each represented by individual circles, how much would your circles overlap? How much do you want your lives to overlap? What is realistic in this stage of life?

All three degrees of involvement can work as long as you agree on the amount of involvement you both desire. Once you understand your expectations and desired involvement, you can set realistic goals for your marriage. Then, to put feet on your goals, answer five questions: what, why, how, when, and what could stop us from achieving our goal? Date Ten will help you take the next step and turn your desires and dreams for your marriage into reality!

Achieving an Intentional Marriage

PART 1: DETERMINE YOUR DEGREE OF INVOLVEMENT

1. Which of the images below best indicates the degree of involvement you have in your marriage right now? Mark an x next to it to indicate your response.

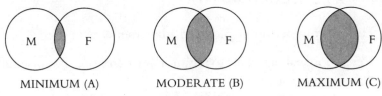

MINIMUM (A)   MODERATE (B)   MAXIMUM (C)

DEGREES OF INVOLVEMENT IN MARRIAGE

2. Which image best describes the degree of involvement you would like to have in your marriage? Circle the image to indicate your response.

3. What degree of involvement is realistic for you in this season of your life? Write the word "realistic" next to the image to indicate your response.

PART 2: SET REALISTIC GOALS

Use the following questions to discuss and set realistic goals for your marriage.

1. Brainstorm possible goals. Consider short- and long-term goals. (See pages 24 and 134–35 for ideas.)

2. Choose one goal to begin with and use the five questions to develop your plan.

    - *What?* (Choose one goal.)

    - *Why?* (Why is this goal important to you?)

- *How?* (What specific steps will you take to reach your goal?)

- *When?* (Write it in your calendar!)

- *What could stop us from achieving our goal?* (Identify potential obstacles and how you might respond to them.)

PART 3: WRITE YOUR DECLARATION OF INTENTION

Write your chosen goal on your Declaration of Intention (next page), then sign and date it. Tear it out and put it where you can see it.

POST-DATE APPLICATION

- Follow your action plan. Make adjustments as needed.

- Keep a journal or a chart to monitor your progress. For instance, "Today we got up ten minutes early for our couple-sharing time. It was so meaningful, we plan to repeat it tomorrow!"

- Keep looking for the positive and complimenting each other.

- Continue your habit of dating. Some couples agree to go back through 10 Great Dates at least once a year.

- Together, make a list of at least three to five future dates you would like to have. See our list of suggested Bonus Dates on pages 149–50. Your marriage will remain alive and healthy as you nurture it.

Achieving an Intentional Marriage

PART 1: DETERMINE YOUR DEGREE OF INVOLVEMENT

1. Which of the images below best indicates the degree of involvement you have in your marriage right now? Mark an x next to it to indicate your response.

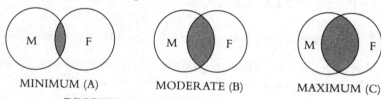

MINIMUM (A)   MODERATE (B)   MAXIMUM (C)
DEGREES OF INVOLVEMENT IN MARRIAGE

2. Which image best describes the degree of involvement you would like to have in your marriage? Circle the image to indicate your response.

3. What degree of involvement is realistic for you in this season of your life? Write the word "realistic" next to the image to indicate your response.

PART 2: SET REALISTIC GOALS

Use the following questions to discuss and set realistic goals for your marriage.

1. Brainstorm possible goals. Consider short- and long-term goals. (See pages 24 and 134–35 for ideas.)

2. Choose one goal to begin with and use the five questions to develop your plan.

   • *What?* (Choose one goal.)

   • *Why?* (Why is this goal important to you?)

- *How?* (What specific steps will you take to reach your goal?)

- *When?* (Write it in your calendar!)

- *What could stop us from achieving our goal?* (Identify potential obstacles and how you might respond to them.)

PART 3: WRITE YOUR DECLARATION OF INTENTION

Write your chosen goal on your Declaration of Intention (next page), then sign and date it. Tear it out and put it where you can see it.

POST-DATE APPLICATION

- Follow your action plan. Make adjustments as needed.

- Keep a journal or a chart to monitor your progress. For instance, "Today we got up ten minutes early for our couple-sharing time. It was so meaningful, we plan to repeat it tomorrow!"

- Keep looking for the positive and complimenting each other.

- Continue your habit of dating. Some couples agree to go back through 10 Great Dates at least once a year.

- Together, make a list of at least three to five future dates you would like to have. See our list of suggested Bonus Dates on page 149–50. Your marriage will remain alive and healthy as you nurture it.

DECLARATION OF INTENTION

Because we want to keep growing in our love for
each other, we will pursue the following:

1. _____

2. _____

_____
HUSBAND

_____
WIFE

_____
DATE